SOCIAL RESEARCH IN RURAL COMMUNITIES

SOCIAL RESEARCH IN RURAL COMMUNITIES

(SECOND EDITION)

P. A. Twumasi
Professor of Sociology and Former Head,
Department of Sociology and Former Dean
Faculty of Social Studies, University of Ghana, Legon

GHANA UNIVERSITIES PRESS
ACCRA
2001

Published by
GHANA UNIVERSITIES PRESS
P. O. BOX GP 4219, ACCRA

Tel: 233 (021) 513401-4,513383
e-mail: ghanauniversitiespress@yahoo.com

First published 1986, Reprinted 1993
Second Edition revised and expanded
© P. A. Twumasi 2001
ISBN: 9964–3–0267–3
Reprinted 2005

Produced in Ghana
Typeset by Ghana Universities Press, Accra
Printed by SuperTrade Complex Limited, Accra.

TO MY WIFE AND CHILDREN

CONTENTS

List of Tables

PREFACE

This book is an outcome of the author's teaching and research experience at the Department of Sociology, University of Ghana, Legon. As a Lecturer in the subject Techniques of Social Research at the undergraduate and at the graduate levels, he had found it necessary to write this book to satisfy a need. The need is particularly felt by students. At the undergraduate level, they wish to know the various stages involved in the research process; but at the graduate level too students have made enquiries as to whether the methodology used by social scientists operating in industrialized areas of the world can be used meaningfully in less industrialized parts of the world. The indication is that there is a need to write this book to specify some of the problems and issues involved in rural social research with particular reference to Ghana. However, it has implications for other developing countries where rural population predominates.

The author received his University education at the University of Ghana, also at McGill and at the University of Alberta, in Canada. At the post graduate level of his education, the author developed a keen interest in research methodology and in the Sociology of Medicine. His first book *Medical Systems in Ghana: A Study in Medical Sociology,* was published by the Ghana Publishing Corporation, Tema, Ghana, in 1975.

This book deals with the stages involved in the process of social research, the problems and issues of fieldwork and it tackles some of the issues the social scientist commonly deals with in less industrialized cultural setting. The author looks at other related issues: whether the social scientist can in fact sharpen his methodology to approximate that of his counterpart in the physical and the biological sciences. He looks at the problem of science: can a discipline claim scientific method if its methods are systematized and have a built-in replication and a good measure of reliability and validity? The social scientists and other scientists in the physical and biological sectors use the scientific method. But social scientists deal with people in their natural environment. They deal with social phenomena, with human beings whose interactive activities are the most varied of all variables. For this reason, social scientists have an extra problem of trying to control many variables of both antecedent and intervening sorts which usually make their work difficult.

After working for the past seven years in rural areas (in various parts in Ghana) one begins to notice the varied nature of the Ghanaian society, its various people, its culture, and other related problems.

How do the people define their social reality? What meanings do they give to their social action? What methods can assist the social investigator to "X-ray" the society and to collect relevant data? In the face of minimal computer services and other research tools, what problems do social scientists face in the research process when they use methodological tools developed by scientists in industrialized society?

These are some of the problems which will direct the orientation of the author. An attempt will also be made to offer some suggestions and to stimulate students in social research to develop a critical approach to the problems of social research. If the student develops the mind for critical thinking, if he acquires the ability to expose the false and if he gets a keen sense of the scientific method, then the student can operate in various social environments.

January 1986   *P. A. Twumasi*
                                                                    Legon

PREFACE TO THE SECOND EDITION

In writing this second edition of *Social Research in Rural Communities,* I have taken into account the interest shown by students, field workers, and by the general public in the first edition. The interest, as I have been informed by the numerous letters, is expressed in the need for decision-makers to base their decisions on reliable and valid information. Such an information base should be obtained from scientific research to help to move us into the scientific era necessary for the technological development of the country.

There is no doubt whatsoever that in all known viable technological societies, scientific discoveries and scientific pathways in the collection of data are *sine qua non* to development. Emotional outbursts and societal myths and beliefs cannot be ignored, but in real scientific development, we must be guided by scientific facts. It is, therefore, axiomatic to say that modern societies' movement and sustainability towards technological growth and development depend on scientific methodology.

In our institutions, we need to understand what is going on, we need to explore new pathways to help us to change for the better and/or to manage change. We need to be concerned with rural development. How then can research work help in the development of our rural society? Research work based on scientific evidence is able to throw light on the existing situation; it can tell us about the existing conditions, the lifestyle of the people and their institutional networks. It is also from research interviews that we are able to get the "feel" of what the people in their own localities think about themselves and their living conditions. It helps policy-makers to get an inside view about our people in order to initiate an effective rapprochement for developing the rural areas.

Students at all levels of the educational stream need to know the stages of social research, they need to appreciate the scientific method of investigation. They need to be conversant with how to outline a research proposal; the cost aspect of social research must be estimated and the field techniques to enable the researcher to collect and analyze data must be worked out.

In this edition, therefore, I have added material on the uses of social research to the conclusion and a new one on the modalities for entering the field. In this age of computers, the research worker must have an insight into computer analysis of the data before he sets out to write the results of his investigation. A brief sketch on the use of computer in data analysis has been provided.

Indeed, I am grateful to the Director of Ghana Universities Press, Mr. K. M. Ganu, and his associates for the great help they have rendered to me in the publication of this second edition. I also give thanks and appreciation to my wife and children for giving me the peace of mind to work on this second edition.

December 1998   *Prof. P. A. Twumasi*

ACKNOWLEDGEMENTS

Scholarship is a cooperative enterprise, and I have made use of the help of several people in the writing and publication of this book. I owe first a debt of gratitude to the Ghana Universities Press for accepting to publish it. I wish to register my deep appreciation to the following for permission to use illustrative articles that appear in the book. They are: Dr. John Sinclair's "Social Mobility and the Characteristics of Students at the University of Ghana", the Editors of *Universitas,* University of Ghana, Legon, for P. A. Twumasi's "A Study of Some Social Characteristics of Ghanaian Medical Students — Towards an Understanding of Medical Socialization" and the Faculty of Social Sciences, University of Cape Coast and Mr. K. M. Ganu for Chapter 6 and the Household Interview Schedule in the latter's MSc Thesis. I also wish to record my acknowledgement of the contribution of various research studies I did with my colleagues.

I am particularly grateful to Professor Kwasi Wiredu for the healthy criticism I received from him. My thanks also go to my graduate and undergraduate students who helped me to realize the need to write the book, especially Mr. A. P. Achampong, a graduate student, who read through the draft; also Miss Georgina Disu who typed the manuscript — to them all, I say: thank you!

As for any errors, substantial or marginal which may be found in the text of the book. I am entirely responsible for them.

Chapter 1

THE NATURE OF SOCIAL RESEARCH

THE PROBLEM

For sometime now, I have been wondering whether some of the methods and concepts used by social scientists in collecting research information among our illiterate peoples are in fact relevant and meaningful in helping us to understand our traditional societies. Many of these concepts and methods have been developed to fit into the style of life in modern industrial societies. The situation we find in the rural traditional setting, where illiteracy prevails, is different. The people operate from a different conceptual frame and level of social consciousness. There is a need, therefore, to critically examine a suitable methodology.

SOCIAL RESEARCH

In Social Research, the scientist goes to get information from the social world. He tries to discover social forms and social processes through a methodology which is systematic and well organized. The social scientist assumes the existence of the social world; he also assumes that the scientific method can be used to gather data from the social world and to know the existing social pattern.

We can discover the nature of the social world, we can understand its organizations, explain some of its crucial parameters and offer some suggestions which can form the basis of prediction. The social world can be studied and analyzed; and meaningful patterns can be discovered. The social world, therefore, is the operational laboratory of the social scientist. It has a well-defined social structure because people do not generally act in a chaotic manner. Rules of social behaviour exist to guide people to act in meaningful ways and to maintain a form of social life. Therefore, we can study human types within well-defined social structures.

Assuming these positions, the social scientist can develop meaningful methods with built-in objectivity to study the nature of the social world so that he can present an intelligible image of the society he is studying. For this reason, the social scientist must be dogma-free. Except for his preoccupation with the notion that the social world exists with a structure and that through scientific investigation, he can discover the social world and what goes on therein.

Social Sciences and Physical Sciences

The social scientist is faced with enormous problems because he is dealing with human beings. His counterpart in the physical sciences works in a laboratory, using relatively well-developed tools and methodological techniques. Thus the most basic difference, between the other sciences and the social sciences is that the former's tools and techniques in data collection tend to be more precise and more accurate in measuring the phenomenon under study. The physical scientist, for example uses refined instruments or aids to observe. The microscope is used to achieve more accurate and in-depth observation, which tends to be highly reliable and valid. The social scientist, on the other hand, has not yet developed comparably reliable and valid tools of measurement. Despite this relative disadvantage of the social scientist in getting accurate data there is nevertheless an area in which he has an advantage over the physical scientist. The social scientist deals with human beings so he can ask his respondents questions; he can check from other human sources to get a meaningful feedback in order to ascertain the true nature of the information. This advantage, if used properly by the investigator, can assist him to check his information and to disentangle truth from falsehood.

Various methods have been devised by the social scientist to check the data he collects. In carrying out a particular research, the investigator employs various methods simultaneously; he may use the participant observation, the interviewing method, the questionnaire methods, records from libraries, archives and museum according to the dictates of his objectives. The social scientist is in a position to check his data through these processes and to detect sources of inconsistencies. These approaches can help the social scientist to collect reliable and valid material comparable to those obtained by physical/biological studies.

THE CONCEPT OF SOCIOLOGY

Many social scientists have looked at the concept of Sociology, its structure, its methods and its functional aspects. The emerging view is that the sociologist is engaged in a wide field in studying human interactive activities. The sociologist is concerned with the product of group activities, the processes of social interaction and of social interactions and of social relationships and how they affect people. The sociologist studies the structures which emerge from the interactive activities. The distinctive aim of the sociological research enterprise, therefore, is to study, to understand, to explain and to make predictions about existing social structures and social relationships.

The concept of a social structure is of crucial significance in the method of the social scientist. It is used as a conceptual and analytical tool. It is a structural pattern of relationships. Without a well-defined social structure, it will be difficult to study societies by the use of scientific method. We need to study the forms of societies, the rules of social behaviour, the existing processes and mechanisms in solving social problems and maintaining social order, how social order is maintained in the face of conflicting ideas. These are some of the general and meaningful questions the sociologist can pursue when he studies structures of societies. More specific questions can be formulated when he gets an inside view of the existing social forms.

According to Biesanz and Biesanz (1969: 33), "all human interaction, the normal as well as the abnormal, the everyday as well as the exciting, is grist for the sociologist's mill." The sociologist is engaged in the search for knowledge and his field is the group's processes and activities; whenever men come together, the sociologist has a natural habitat to study the forms and the processes of interaction.

Pitirim Sorokin (1962), famous sociologist, argues that Sociology must concern itself with the study of the generic properties of social interaction. In other words, it is not the fact that there are three persons in a given social situation or gathering that interests the sociologist, but rather what happens as a result of their social interaction. The relationship is social and this is the essence of sociological enterprise. Sociology is the study of meaningful social interaction and how tangible social interaction and social situations influence social living and the state of the mind of the individual.

Durkheim (1966) mentions that the group affects the individual's actions in meaningful ways. The group, in the Durkheimian sense, is the basic unit, the generic unit, the true sociological laboratory in which social facts are produced. Social facts, according to Durkheim, are produced by the human group in interaction activities. The sociologist focuses on people in groups, on their activities, on human types, on institutions, and on social relationships. The sociologist must ask searching questions about the group. For example, what sustains its existence? Why does it persist or dissolve? What are some of the processes involved in initiating changes? And he seeks answers to his questions through the scientific method.

THE SCIENTIFIC METHOD

The social scientist works in that part of the human environment which is susceptible to experience by man. He recognizes the existence of the total universe of man, with its diverse specification of subject matter and issues of public concern, but can only operate within those variables which can be studied through the scientific method.

Science is a way of approaching the empirical world, the world which can be studied by using an observable method. Science has limitations, it does not aim at persuasion; it aims at objectivity in its effort to gather meaningful knowledge from the empirical world. In this approach, the scientist gathers data through an organized method; then he analyzes his data by using analytical concepts and categories which are logically derived from his conceptual model and from his stated hypotheses.

Science abstracts from reality. The abstracted concepts are the tools of science. They are the language of the scientist which can assist him to study social phenomena, to build models about social reality, and to possess the power of communication. They must have special meaning and applicability. They must not just arouse a feeling but must be so constructed that all their components are clearly defined and analytically distinct.

Scientific Concepts

The concepts of science must be defined in exact and precise terms. To carry out any scientific project, it is the work of the scientist to select his concepts and to define them operationally. It is necessary to note that the concepts must be logically derived from a theoretical orientation. From theory, concepts are selected and defined empirically. When empirical definitions are made, the scientist can begin to focus on his area of study and make the necessary observation.

The student of science is introduced to concepts and helped to formulate concepts, to define them and to use conceptual frameworks. Blalock (1960: 8) mentions that the moment one begins to design a research project which aims to test a proposition within a framework of theory, it becomes evident that a number of things must be done before the test can be made and the specific concepts defined theoretically and empirically. For example, if we say that the socio-economic status of a person determines his level of social consciousness, we must define what we mean by the term "socio-economic status." For this definition, the researcher must be familiar with the existing notions and definitions (see Fig. 1).

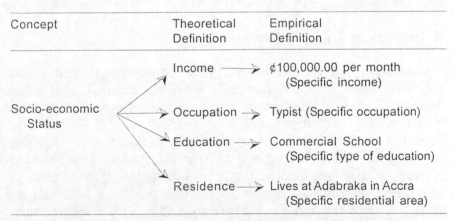

Concept	Theoretical Definition	Empirical Definition
	Income ⟶	¢100,000.00 per month (Specific income)
Socio-economic Status	Occupation ⟶	Typist (Specific occupation)
	Education ⟶	Commercial School (Specific type of education)
	Residence ⟶	Lives at Adabraka in Accra (Specific residential area)

Fig. 1: Relationship between the Theoretical and Empirical Definitions of a Concept.

The definition in Fig. 1 shows the variants of the variable, socio-economic status. These have been defined theoretically and empirically. The theoretical definitions are necessary but not sufficient to help the empirically-minded social scientist to operate and to collect data. For him the definitions must be stated in operational terms to direct his observation and analysis. In social research, we begin with conceptual frames, then we derive empirical indicators, which must be defined clearly. In the above example, the empirical indicator of income is the actual take-home pay of the person or the respondent. If the respondent receives ¢100,000.00 a month then this amount is used operationally to indicate his income.

Such definitions can spell out the specific ways in which the researcher can collect and measure his data. In science, therefore, the conceptual and operational definitions must be clear; we must avoid vague and ambiguous definitions. Definitions must be identified in mutually exclusive and exhaustive ways. Precision is necessary in operationalization of a variable to allow reliable and valid measurement, so that other social scientists can use similar procedures to achieve similar results. In carrying out fieldwork, the actual test of science, therefore, is to define clearly the conceptual variables. If, for example, there are two distinct definitions, as argued by Blalock, the researcher must know that he is faced with the test of two distinct concepts. Science is an intellectual endeavour, its *raison d'etre* is to make an attempt to present an intelligible image of the phenomena under study and to explain their relations through the creation of well-defined concepts.

Objectivity in Social Science

In the scientific world, the scientist must be objective. He must be critical in his attitude and must take a neutral stand. The scientist must be humble enough to accept the facts of the situation and must be willing to change his original stand in the face of tested and valid new facts. There is a built-in-humility in science, which gives durability to the scientific enterprise. It gives to science the ability to correct its knowledge, to progress and to discover the "truth". In achieving this objectivity, the social scientist must examine his own basic assumptions and free his research design from the traces of subjective feeling and personal biases.

It is difficult, in many instances, to achieve a high degree of objectivity in social studies. This problem has occupied the minds of many social scientists. Because the scientist deals with human beings and he many have his own predispositions and loyalties, so the argument goes, he may be biased. He may accept a particular group's view point, thus, clouding his objectivity.

In carrying out social research, the social investigator must adhere to objectivity. As said earlier, in dealing with human situation, the scientist must keep away from subjective alliances. He does this by stating his problem clearly from the start. The statement of the problem must be done in a neutral form. Then he must collect data from all sections of the community. The information so gathered must be examined and taken into account in arriving at conclusions. In so doing, the social scientist will be able to collect reliable data from the field. And he will be able to take a neutral stand in the collection of the information as well as in his analysis.

On the above issue, there are two schools of thought as far as objectivity in the social sciences is concerned. One school says that the social scientist can never be objective; the other school argues that the social scientist can achieve objectivity if he tries hard by continuing to search for appropriate methodological tools and measurement indices in collecting and processing his data. The latter position gives the scientist the confidence he needs to search for methods and procedures to be used to collect reliable and valid data. We need to search critically for appropriate methods. The issue is that social reality exists. The social scientist must find appropriate methods to X-ray this social reality. We need not give up in desperation because our methods are sometimes questionable. We must continue with the search to get reliable and valid tools of measurement.

In scientific work, the researcher must be able to distinguish between a phenomenon which can be studied by the application of scientific method and that which cannot be studied by the canons of scientific method. In order to make this distinction the research scientist must find out whether the social situation is in fact observable, whether it can be described and measured and whether it can show some form of regularity and variability.

For humanistic reasons, the methodology of the social scientist is slow to develop because human beings cannot be easily subjected to rigorous scientific experiments of the animal laboratory type. It is also difficult for the research scientist to carry out a longitudinal study at times on human subjects for long periods of time. It is difficult because if one were to follow all the stages of human interaction, one may not have the time and the energy to study the group. Also it is difficult because the human situation changes so rapidly. The research worker may even die in the process. The point is, unlike cats and dogs and other experimental animals and objects, human beings have longer life spans. At times, as ideology may play a part in retarding the progress of social science, many research workers tend to be ideologically committed and hope to see only what they set out to see or what they want to achieve. They fail to follow the basic canons of the scientific method. The student of science must adopt a critical outlook to avoid this negative position. There is the need for the scientist to achieve a significant degree of objectivity by using viable methods in the collection and in the analysis of data. There is also the need to sharpen the scientific method in order to detect errors in organized ways.

Objectivity is a very important subject matter in social science research methodology. The questions the student of social science method must pursue are: How objectivity in social science can be achieved? What factors are essential in maximizing objectivity in social sciences?

In all social sciences, the individual's characteristics and idiosycracies play an essential part in the selection of topics for "research study". The methods used in the collection of data are essentially the device of the researcher. From these beginnings, therefore, personal attitudes and wishes tend to colour the data collection processes if great care is not taken to keep out subjective biases.

How then do we keep off subjectivity in the collection of data? We need to design a model for the entire research process. The stages in the research design must be followed. The measuring tools as well as the research questions, if any, must be pretested. The wording must be clearly framed and understood by the local people. If the researcher employs the services of research assistants, he must train them to keep away from subjective biases and attitudes. They must be trained to keep to the methods designed for the collection of data so that the information gathered can be worthwhile to achieve a high degree of reliability and validity in the measurement. If, for example, we need to find out the attitudes of people with regard to family planning, questions must be included to determine whether the respondents are answering the questions in an honest way. Such built-in questions are meant to check falsehood as well as unreliable answers. For example, the researcher may ask a question: Do you like to have a small or a large family? If the answer is for a *small family,* then what will be your attitude towards those who wish to have a large family? Here, the response is expected to be unfavourable. But, if he is favourably disposed to large families, the researcher can detect that a contradictory statement has been made. It denotes falsehood in the answer.

It is also possible to impose one's own expectation on the person who is answering the question. Personal attitudes and non-seriousness must be kept away from contaminating the expected (objective) answers. In other words, the field researcher must be neutral in his or her own interaction with the interviewee.

Objectivity in social science, therefore, deals with issues of ethics and politics of research methods. Ethics and politics in research design are often closely intertwined. Ethics in this usage deals more with the methods employed while political issues are more concerned with the selection of the topic with the substance and the use of the research study. Since researchers are humans, it is difficult to ignore the subjective tendencies which may occur in the research process.

The data collection methods and the results of the research must be replicable by other researchers in order to accept the reliability and validity of the measurement. To achieve this, personal values and views must be set aside for the duration of the research. The classical statement on objectivity and neutrality in social science is Max Weber's lecture on "Science as a Vocation". In his statement, Weber developed the concept of "value free sociology". He had argued that sociology and other social science subjects must not be encumbered by personal values if the social scientist was to make a special contribution to society (Weber 1956: 231).

For further exposition of this topic, students, especially graduate students may see (Babbie 1982(a), 1982(b); Cole 1980; Boruch and Cecil 1979; and Weber 1956).

THEORY AND RESEARCH

The scientific method of investigation goes beyond the detection of a problem and the mere collection of unconnected facts. It is theoretical in its orientation; it abstracts from reality for the purposes of generalization. The method or approach is systematically controlled and research is set against an existing body of theory. Theoretical orientation, therefore, is a very important aspect in social research. A theory is a coherent group of general propositions used to explain phenomena.

There is a basic inter-relationship between theory and research. Without theory, the social researcher will not be able to operate effectively; his data collection techniques will be sterile. The notion of what data to collect emerges precisely from theoretical position. Popular opinion usually conceives of theory and research as if the two were opposed to each other. Theory should not be confused with mere abstraction or speculation. The social scientist needs a body of theory to construct his research model and to guide his analysis.

If we look closely at what the social scientist does and how he operates we can see specifically that there is a basic and intricate relationship between theory and social research. Theory and empirical research are complementary; they are not diamentrically opposed, the two are intertwined. Theory is an important tool in any scientific endeavour because of the following facts: theory defines the orientation of the subject matter by assisting to locate the type of data that can be abstracted. It looks at reality and helps us to understand the nature of its inter-relationship. It assists the researcher to develop a conceptual model by which the relevant social phenomena can be classified in a systematic fashion; and it helps us to explain the phenomena under study.

From another point of view, theories can be tested in a field to assess whether they are relevant in a particular social setting. If the theories so tested cannot stand the empirical findings one can initiate theoretical argument from his empirical findings. Theories have major functions; they narrow the range of facts to be studied by the scientist. They help to define what kinds of facts are meaningful and what are pertinent to the research design. Theories can help to explain relationships and to organize research data in a meaningful conceptual frame.

If knowledge is to be organized, then there must be a system to impose some form of logic and structure on it. Theories are important in this systematization of knowledge. They help to classify knowledge. From theory, we derive concept; for example, the concepts of a society, of social class, of socialization, of social mobility, of stratification and of social distance are derived from a body of theories. They are used to examine reality, to explain and to predict social situations. In every known society, as indicated in Fig. 2, the introduction of new ideas can lead to social change. In social research, the specific ideas must be observed and deviations from such positions can then be explained. This illustrates the point that behind an empirical generalization is a body of theories. Theory states that under specific X conditions we can observe Y. The existing conditions must be described, analyzed and explained; while new hypotheses or tentative propositions are derived and tested in the empirical setting.

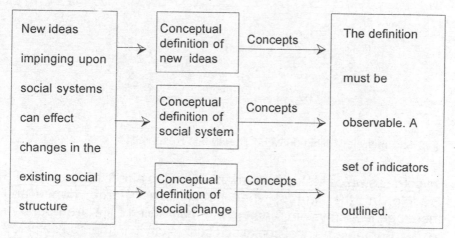

Fig. 2: Theoretical Stance and its Relationship to Empirical World.

Fig. 3 shows the nature of the interrelationship between theory and research. In the research process, the researcher must be guided by theory and in a logical fashion, hypothesis is derived from the theory. It is from this process that specific concepts are obtained and clearly defined as empirical observational tools to aid data collection process. Thereafter, when the information (data) is gathered, the researcher must process the data based on the basic ideas derived from the theory he or she is working from. As shown in the diagram, there is a basic interrelationship between theory and research. This is the method of science. It must also be stressed that the concepts so derived from the theory and/or the hypothesis must be clearly defined in an empirical way to aid observation.

Fig. 2 can aid the student to understand (Fig. 3). For example, new ideas can affect changes in a social system. In this context, urbanism states a theoretical position in the area of social change. The student can, therefore, derive logically from the theory, a

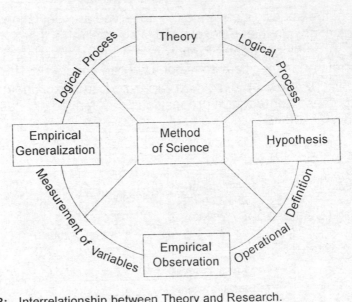

Fig. 3:   Interrelationship between Theory and Research.

hypothesis which states that urbanization can affect the lifestyle of a people. In other words, when people live in large, dense and heterogeneous system, changes in their style of life are bound to occur. For the empirical social scientist, a city can then be selected for comparative purpose to observe the difference between rural (village) and urban (city) living.

STAGES IN A RESEARCH DESIGN

Selecting a Research Problem

The initial problem any research scientist is faced with is how to select a research problem. There are four major concerns which are relevant in the selection of a research problem. Firstly, the research scientist must perceive a problem. This is perhaps the most difficult consideration in the process of selecting a problem. Cohen and Nagel (1934) comment that the ability to perceive in some experiences the occasion for a problem and especially, a problem whose solution has a bearing on the solution of other problems is not a common talent among men. They go on to point out that it is a mark of scientific genius to be sensitive to difficulties where less gifted people are untroubled by doubt. In many cases the research scientist needs to think about the general problem area by reading from on-going literature and in the subject area of his interest. Secondly, he can acquire the requisite information through discussion with his colleagues and other knowledgeable people. This will enable him to know the general area of his problem. Once the student has chosen or formulated a problem, he must read widely to get acquainted with the nuances of the problem in a systematic and a reasonable manner. Relevant information must be collected from books, newspaper articles, documents, archival materials etc., and proper acknowledgement must be given. The scientist compiles a bibliographical index on his readings. The student of science must become aware of what has been accomplished in his area of study. He becomes acquainted with field methods and gets an insight into the modes of analysis. Thirdly, he must reduce the problem to a manageable size. This is an essential step in the process of social research. The inexperienced student of social science often selects too large, at times, too general a topic. Fourthly, the inherent indicators or variables must be defined and the objectives of the study must be stated clearly.

The theoretical significance of the problem must be considered. The research must be a worthwhile exercise; it must be such as could increase and update our knowledge.

Definition of Concepts and Variables

There is also the need to clarify the basic concepts and analytical variable. This process will help the investigator to define the abstract concepts empirically as operational indicators. Clarity of definition is an essential aspect of social research. There must be some systematic and socially relevant means of applying the abstract concepts to some specific observable events in order to carry out meaningful research.

Thus, the researcher must develop or decide upon some procedure by which he can proceed to define the concepts. Let us assume that we are studying "status differential in a community." We must devise a method to help us to measure the concept "status". How do we define or get specific empirical indicators of "status"? The definition must be relevant and pertinent to the existing notions. How do we define persons in various social positions? Do we classify individuals on the basis of such variables as income, occupations, education and residence? We need to know the specific empirical indexes used by the people within the society we are studying. If we are clear on the prevailing norms of the society, then we can begin to define empirically the abstract concepts. One way to achieve a reasonable and significant definition is to do a preliminary study to find out how the people themselves define the concepts. What criteria do they use in assessing or in categorizing people in the community? Resultant definitions must be acceptable to the community in terms of usage, relevancy, clarity and applicability.

Selecting Objectives

How do we go about collecting data to achieve the aims of study? The aims of the study must be outlined. They direct the scientist to find answers to the main research problem.

It must be remembered in this regard that, in selecting objectives, the main research topic must be logically divided into sub-topics. These sub-topics must be logically derived from the main research problem. Let us give an example. My interest was to study the place of traditional medicine within the society. My objectives were to find out

(1) What is the place of traditional medicine?
(2) What is the rationale behind the practice of traditional medicine?
(3) What role does it play in the society?
(4) What type of organizational base supports traditional medicine and why?
(5) In what circumstances do the sick prefer traditional medicine?
(6) What aspects of traditional medicine have undergone changes? (See Twumasi 1975).

Let us look at another example of the selection of objectives. The research focus was to find out some of the social and demographic characteristics of Ghanaian Medical Students, from 1964 to 1974, to assist medical planners and policy makers to get a background knowledge about the type of students who enter the University of Ghana Medical School (See Twumasi 1975).

The objectives were stated in terms of the following questions:

(1) What are some of the background characteristics of the Ghanaian Medical Students?
    (a) Where do they come from?
    (b) What is the age distribution?
    (c) What is the sex pattern?
(2) What are some of their aims and aspirations?
(3) What sort of problems and issues emerge during their medical socialization?

These objectives serve as useful directives for the research. It is from these objectives that the research questions are derived. If one intends to use a questionnaire method, or an interviewing technique in the collection of one's field data, one needs to raise specific questions from each of the stated objectives.

Conceptual Model or Research Design

The research design starts with a conceptual model or hypothesis. The conceptual model is a set of theoretical ideas, hunches or clearly-defined concepts to direct the scientist in his research operation. The model is a tentative statement concerning some of the expectations of the investigator. It states a tentative casual relationship between two variables: dependent and independent factors. It asserts that if a particular occurrence happens then another predicted one will follow. For example, in the design, it may be stated: "the higher a person's social status, the lower his prejudice towards aliens". The two crucial variables are social status and prejudice. That is to say, if we know the social position of a person, we can determine his level of prejudice. The crucial variables must then be defined.

    The researcher can also start with series of hypotheses or a set of specific objectives. For the uninitiated in social research, a word of caution is necessary on hypothesis. A hypothesis serves as a tentative guide to help locate and examine data. It must not be held as the gospel truth. One should not allow oneself to be tempted into thinking that the hypothesis is proven without field data. The data collected must be critically examined to confirm or to negate the original hypothesis. Let us give an example from Nukunya and Twumasi (1975) financed by Population Dynamic Programme. The stated hypotheses were:

(1) The utilization of traditional and modern methods of heal-

ing is a function of availability.

(2) Those living near modern hospitals are more likely to make frequent use of hospitals.

(3) In the realm of psychological ills, people will tend to frequent traditional medical practitioners.

The hypotheses served only as guides which directed the research and the analysis of data. The data was followed patiently and analytically. In the final analysis, some of the hypotheses were confirmed. A few of the hypotheses were not confirmed by the available data and were rejected.

As argued by Riley (1964: 10–14), models are important aspects of the research design because they serve as the organizing image of the phenomena one is studying in the real social world. In her *Sociological Research,* Matilda Riley outlined these points to be considered in building a sociological model:

(1) People must be identified in their collectivities;

(2) The aspects of their behaviour or the properties to be studied must be clarified;

(3) The ways by which these aspects fit together and affect each other must be cautioned; that is to say, the investigator would wish to find out the relationship among a set of social variables and other structural properties. The model, therefore, is an essential component in any scientific enterprise.

Research Procedure

In any research design, we must include, among other things, the techniques to be used in the collection of the field materials. We must include the sampling techniques and the analytical categories.

The stages involved in outlying a final research design must include:

(1) Specification of the research problem;

(2) A thorough review of the literature;

(3) Specification of the study's objectives or the hypotheses;

(4) The sample area;

(5) The techniques for collecting the data;

(6)   The analytical categories or the pertinent variables to be used in the analysis of data; and

(7)   The budget; i.e. how much the research will cost.

An Example of a Research Design

The author was asked by the National Council on Women and Development to study women's health problems in rural Ghana. First, he stated the problem and outlined his objectives. The following research design was the outcome.

Introduction

Ghanaian women have been recognized in various studies as performing important social and economic functions. They are found in many trading activities. They also manage their homes, care for their children and supplement the income of their household.

For these reasons, they are faced with many physical and psychological hazards. It has also been noted that a significant proportion of women live and work in rural and outlying settlements in Ghana. It is precisely in these areas that medical care facilities and personnel are lacking. Insanitary conditions, superstition, malnutrition (to name only a few things) tend to act as predisposing factors in the causation of many infectious diseases. The result is that many women are beset with various health problems.

Objectives

(1)   What types of health problems face the women in rural   areas?

(2)   What are some of the specific diseases?

(3)   What measures do they take to find a cure?

(4)   What factors determine the type and choice of available health facilities?

A study of this nature would furnish us with the supporting facts and figures to enable us to know rural women's health conditions and health care utilization pattern. Basing the study in a typical rural area, we should be able to get an insight into some of the health conditions of Ghanaian rural women.

Sample

A group of rural villages in the Ashanti Akim administrative district in Ashanti was selected. Households were selected on the basis of the probability sample theory. The respondents were female heads of households. The villages were farming and cocoa-growing settlements.

Data Collection Techniques

(1) Specific questions were used through participant observation and interviews. Through the technique of participant observation and interviewing, the author sought information about patients who attend clinics and those who go to herbalists.

(2) Records were examined to determine frequency, types and nature of disease. The records of health statistics in the nearby clinic or health post were examined.

(3) Case studies and life histories were derived from selected patients to get a firm insight.

The analysis looked at central themes, types of disease, frequency and utilization of health facilities.

Budget

1.	Six Research Assistants at ¢200,000.00 per month for 3 months	= ¢	3,600,000.00
2.	Night allowance of ¢50,000.00 a month for 6 Research Assistants	=	900,000.00
3.	Stationery	=	1,000,000.00
4.	Typist at ¢150,000.00 for 2 months	=	300,000.00
5.	Data Processing for a month	=	500,000.00
6.	Computer Analyst	=	500,000.00
7.	Principal Research Investigator	=	3,000,000.00
8.	Contingency	=	2,000,000.00
	Total		¢11,800,000.00

This is an example of a research design. It is a field plan in which the various research steps and field budget were specified. It is of great assistance for the research scientist to possess a research design to give structure and logic to what he intends to do. From this format, one is able to check errors in a systematic and organized way.

Chapter 2

SAMPLING TECHNIQUES

INTRODUCTION

Sampling technique is important in any social research. The issues involved are: How wide a coverage is acceptable? What types of respondents will be able to give answers to the research questions? Will the selected group of respondents be adequately representative of the community? What typical groups of respondents are available? Can we select a typical village or a community? All these are relevant questions which come to mind when an investigator begins to select a sampling design.

SAMPLING DESIGN

In considering a sampling design, the research scientist first of all determines his population universe. He must be able to outline the parameters of the population he wants to study. Kish (1967) mentions that the first step in the selection of a sample is to consider a sampling design. It denotes all the stages and the processes involved in reaching the respondents. In this area, we must indicate clearly the characteristics of the population. What are the units under consideration? Who are the people in the system? Are they homogenous or heterogeneous group of individuals? Are they predominatly males or females? What are some of the background characteristics of the population? These questions will enable the research scientist to have an idea about the existing social situation. An intelligible idea about the parameters of the population can help the investigator to determine the type of sampling design. If a group is a heterogeneous one in terms of its social characteristics, there is the need to include more individuals and to stratify the group in order to lower variance. In this case, stratification means putting individuals in common groups. There is also the need to know the types of institutions which exist in the community. All units of the institutions must be represented, if they are relevant to the aims and objectives of the research. For example, in a hospital study, the types of clinics and other health agencies were considered in the sample selection; the types of personnel who work in these agencies or clinics were included. A time limit was also imposed on the selection of the sample. The consideration is essentially a pragmatic one, i.e. it was necessary to specify how much me was available to the researcher. Consideration of this sort constitutes an important element in sample selection.

There are two types of sampling techniques: probability sampling and non-probability sampling. These two sampling techniques are used in various research studies. For this reason, it is relevant to discuss these sampling techniques and to indicate how they can be used in social research.

Probability Sampling

In probability sampling, each and every unit within the population is given an equal chance of being selected. The designer must have a selection design and an estimation procedure. In studying a particular community, the research workers goes to the community. He maps the area under study. Mapping means that the investigator must get to know the outlay of the community's boundary. He must be acquainted with the community and all its principal dimensions. The mapping may be done by the investigator with the help of some knowledgeable people from the community. He can also obtain the area map from the Town Council or District Assembly. In Ghana and many other developing countries, an up-to-date map may be difficult to locate. It is, therefore, not advisable to rely solely on official maps. After mapping, the houses are numbered with each house having an equal chance of being selected. It is necessary for the research investigator to approach probability sampling techniques with caution. Firstly, he must take into account all the elements or, in this case, the individuals within the area of study. For example, in a household survey all the household must be given equal chance of inclusion. Secondly, he must decide on the method of selection (how many individuals or household heads the research can accommodate). At times, it is advisable to seek help from a statistician well-versed in sampling techniques.

After the houses have been counted and numbered serially, sample size is then determined. This aspect is based on both theoretical and practical considerations. In sampling theory, the larger the sample size, the more likely it is to approximate the true images of the population. In other words, the idea is to select a representative sample whose mean($\bar{x}$) approximates the population mean. The difference between sample $\bar{x}$ and the population(μ) is an error. In all serious scientific work, the investigator develops sampling strategies to enable him to get nearer to the true image of the population universe and to avoid substantial error. Thus when the population value and the sampling value are estimated, the difference must be nil or if there is any difference, the difference must not be significant. Any difference is a known error, which arises as a result of inadequate sampling procedures. The survey objectives are important determinants in the selection of a sample size.

The pragmatic aspect of sampling is to determine the practical problems involved in the research, the cost, time and energy. Though they are practical problems, they are very relevant to sampling size determination. The total cost of the research is an important factor. The cost of a research is determined by the time to be spent on it and the number of research personnel the investigator can employ. The time to be spent on a research is also determined by the practical problems involved in the research which include the accessibility of the location and attitude of respondents. These must be taken into consideration before any sample size is determined.

Types of Probability Sampling
We shall now discuss the commonly used types of probability sampling: (1) simple random sampling (2) stratified sampling (3) systematic sampling and (4) cluster sampling.

Simple Random Sampling
By definition, simple random sampling takes into account the fact that all the elements or individuals in the population get equal chance of selection. The investigator must give numbers to all the elements in the selected area. The basic assumption underlying simple random sampling is that the elements or the individuals in the population, are judged to be homogeneous. The individuals, for example, have similar characteristics or attributes. If the investigator wishes to study the student population at Legon, he may classify them as a homogeneous group in terms of the fact that they are students. He may wish to study the views of students towards the university administration or teaching. For this reason, he gives each student at Legon an equal chance of selection, by assigning each one a

number. Then he determines his sample size (in population of 1000 students a sample size of 300 students would be an adequate representation).

The numbers are put into a container and mixed. An assistant may be blindfolded and asked to pick numbers from the container. When he reaches the required sample size, he stops picking from the container. The picked numbers form the basis of the sample. The selection is, thus, based on chance in which the assistant selects or picks the numbers which fall at hand till he reaches the required sample size. This might be laborious. If the sample is large, a more scientific approach is to use a table of random numbers.

The Use of a Table of Random Numbers

The important issue in the selection process is to determine the homogeneity of the unit. That is to say, all the elements in the unit or in the area for the study have similar characteristics. Once this important issue in randomization selection is determined, then each element now has an equal chance of being selected. There should not be a selection bias. Fairness must prevail. With such consideration, the researcher decides upon probability sampling by using a table of random numbers.

The researcher assigns a single number to each element in the list without skipping any number in the total population. It is called the table of random numbers. The researcher then uses it to select elements for the sample. If the sampling frame is in a machine readable form, for example, computer disc or magnetic tape, a simple random sample can be selected automatically by the computer. In effect, the computer programme numbers the elements in the table. It generates its own series of random numbers and points out the list of elements selected.

Suppose the researcher wants to select a simple random sample of 100 people out of a total population of 980. To begin, he numbers the members in the population, from 1 to 980. The next step is to determine the number of digits needed in the random numbers. Since there are 980 members in the population the researcher will need 3 digits, to give everyone a chance of selection. Thus, the range is from 001 to 980. Start with a number by closing your eyes to pick it. That number can be used to select the others (at that interval) till the required size is obtained. If 10, then the next number is 20, 30, etc. The table of random numbers is the sampling frame list from which a probability sample is selected.

The list may be obtained from a school, a district assembly or from a Government agency, etc. The sample members is determined by chance alone and not upon the researcher's judgement which tends to introduce bias.

Stratified Sampling

In stratified sampling, the sampler divides the population into homogeneous units. That is to say, if the sampler has any reason to believe that the population has many dissimilar elements or individuals, he may wish to put similar elements or individuals in one group. For example, in a community study, there may be many ethnic groups. The researchers may wish to obtain views from each ethnic group. For this reason, before he adopts the random sampling procedure, he divides the community into ethnic groups. The final selection principle means that each ethnic group will be represented in the total sample.

Stratification is used to help to lower known variances in the population. The entire community or population is divided into meaningful strata on the basis of the objectives of the study. Within each stratum, a separate sample is taken by using the technique of randomization. From each stratum, the sampler selects the required sample size. The selected individuals or elements are then properly weighted to form a combined estimate for the entire sample size.

Suppose one wishes to study the University of Ghana population. He divides the area into homogeneous units, i.e. the students, lecturers and administrative units. From each group, he must know how many are there. In each unit, each person must be given an equal chance of selection. If the researcher is aware of the total number in each unit, then he will be able to determine an appropriate sample size. For example, if there are 1000 lecturers, it may be convenient to take a sample size of 1/3. It may also be relevant for him to determine a sampling fraction for the three sampling units: the students, lecturers and the administrators. That is to say, he may wish, after knowing the actual numerical strength of each unit, to take 1/3 from each unit.

From each unit, he selects the required sample size and adds the three unit sizes together to form the final selected sample size. The stratification principle could be based on a simple criterion or a combination of two or more criteria. For example, a group may be divided into three homogeneous units on the basis of ethnicity (single criterion), or the basis of the stratification may be due to ethnicity and sex (those coming from a particular ethnic group and being males may be put in one group *et cetera*).

Stratification contributes to sampling efficiency by lowering variance. In this case, we sample homogeneous units. In drawing this type of sample, in some cases, there is the need to consider proportionate representation. For example, if in a given community, there are 100 Moslems, 300 Catholics and 600 Protestants, the investigator may include the representations proportionately. It means that each religious group must be considered and given relevant sampling weighting. If one Moslem is taken, then 3 Catholics will be taken; also for every 1 Catholic taken 2 Protestants should be included. Let us suppose for illustrative purposes that the total sample size is 333. We need to get a sample fraction to select Moslems, Catholics and Protestants. So we may agree on a sample fraction of 1/3 for each group. If we take 1/3 for the Moslem group, we get 33, for the Catholics, we get 100, and for the Protestants, we get 200. The final selection in each stratum is arrived at by the simple random sampling method. In the final analysis, the sub-units estimates have been weighted proportionately and added to form the final combined unit for the entire religious group.

Systematic Sampling

Like the other methods already described, systematic sampling is a version of probability sampling. Its own character is that the unit in the population must be arranged serially and then the selection will be started by finding a random number to begin with. For example, a researcher may decide to study the background of medical students. He calls at the Registry to examine the files before selecting his sample. The files of students, are numbered serially. Knowing the total number of the medical students, he determines his sample size. If there are less than a thousand files, it is appropriate for him to select a sample size of not less than 1/3. Then he cuts pieces of paper and writes down such numbers as 1 2 3 4 5 6 7 8 9 10. He mixes these numbers up to give each number an equal chance of selection. He places them in a container and decides to pick the number that falls at hand. Let us suppose that he picks the number 5. With this number, he selects every 5th file, i.e. 5, 10, 15 etc. till he reaches the sample size he requires. If he gets around 300 files that would be a sufficient sample size. In this connection, the relevant points to consider are: (a) there is an assumption of homogeneity; (b) a random procedure is used to select the starting number in the selection process; and (c) the units are numbered serially.

It is often used in large sample surveys and household surveys. It is perhaps one of the most commonly used selection procedures in conducting large scale survey studies. Its main principle is that the researcher takes every Nth sampling unit after a random start till he reaches the required sample size.

Let us take an illustrative sample. In conducting a large scale survey, the houses in the town must be numbered serially, then through random numbers the required houses are selected to meet the estimated sample size. During a study by Boateng and Twumasi (Community Health Report No. 6, Medical School 1972), the authors used the systematic sampling method. We selected three communities in Accra: Achimota Village, Adabraka and Tesano. The objective was to investigate community health problems and housing types. We divided the survey area into three homogeneous units (Tesano, Adabraka and Achimota Village). We numbered the houses serially in each of the selected areas. Each area was treated as a separate sampling unit. Once the homogeneous units were demarcated, we obtained a random number to begin the selection process. The random number in this case was 10; therefore, every 10th house was selected till we arrived at the required size. In the selected houses, we interviewed all adults above the age of fifteen. The point to be remembered in this regard is that once the homogeneous units are demarcated, the researcher can resort to systematic sampling to arrive at the final selection point.

Cluster Sampling
Cluster sampling is the technique whereby the researcher selects a group of units from groups of similar units as a first stage in sampling. By definition, the term "cluster" means a number of units or elements of the same kind. For example, in large scale surveys, the researcher may identify areas inhabited by people from the same socio-economic background. In a particular city there may be similar areas where the elites reside. Each area is identified as a cluster. In Accra, we may identify Labone Estate, Roman Ridge and Airport Residential Area as examples of high class residential area. Each is a cluster.

In using this technique, therefore, all the high class residential areas must be identified and through the simple random sampling method a specific residential area is selected. After the selection of the specific area, the researcher may decide to use all the houses in the area or resort to the systematic method to select some of the houses.

Kish (1967) points out that when individual selection of elements seems too expensive, survey tasks can be facilitated by selection of clusters. The first step is to identify a cluster unit. For example, in sampling a city, clusters can be identified by following the established residential arrangement. Residential patterns follow a socio-economic arrangement. Usually, people within a given socio-economic status tend to live in cluster areas. It is also necessary to note that within Ghanaian traditional societies, for example, residential clusters can be located on well-defined lines. In certain areas, people from a particular ethnic group tend to live together. If this arrangement can be identified then meaningful clusters can be mapped.

We can also select school pupils by using their classes as cluster units. In a junior school, one class may be selected. After this selection, the researcher may go through the simple random sampling method to select some pupils from the class or he may use the systematic sampling method to make his final selection. This is one reason why some authors argue that in the cluster sampling procedure we go through a multi-stage sampling technique to select the final respondents.

In cluster sampling, the procedure is inexpensive i.e. it is time saving but it is possible to make more errors in this method than in the other method such as the systematic, stratified and simple random procedure. That is to say, the final selection may not be highly representative of the entire population.

Non-Probability Sampling

In non-probability sampling procedure, there is no known way of estimating sampling errors. The method means that the selected sample is not representative of the population because the units in the population are not given the chance to be included in the sample. The procedure does not call for any systematic sampling design. The researcher decides to take what he thinks is the representative unit of the group.

He may decide to choose what he thinks to be a typical village, or a typical informant, or a typical household. This procedure is useful in so far as the researcher knows the area and is aware of the objectives of his study and is also aware of how much error he is able to deal with. Many social scientists use the non-probability sampling to gain preliminary knowledge of the area of study, especially if they are new research workers. In pre-testing or in pilot studies, researchers may resort to non-probability type of sampling. In other words, depending on the nature of the project and on how much error he is able to accommodate, the researcher can use the non-probability sampling technique. It is worth noting that in non-probability type of sampling, it is very difficult for the researcher to calculate errors in a scientific way and one cannot make any meaningful generalization.

Types of Non-probability Sampling
We shall now consider three types of non-probability sampling: (1) accidental sampling, (2) purposive sampling and (3) quota sampling.

Accidental Sampling
This type of non-probability sampling technique is commonly used by journalists and by people engaged in pilot studies. One goes to the field to get whoever is available. The researcher takes a certain sampling size to interview and to obtain information. He may also consider those who are willing to be interviewed. This raises all types of questions. Why were they willing? What type of respondent were they? What type of information are they willing to give? Why are some respondents not willing to be interviewed? Those interviewees are like a captive audience. There is a built-in bias in the information they give. It is quite clear that the respondents in this type of sampling procedure cannot be representative of the community's opinions and views.

Purposive Sampling
As the name implies, the researcher, adhering to the objectives of the study, selects respondents who can answer his research questions. With good calculation and a relevant research strategy, he can pick the respondents he wants to be included in his sample. He selects cases that are judged to typify the views of the group. But it is difficult to know, without explicitly stated criteria, how to determine typicalities. The purposive sample is used in impressionistic studies, in pilot and pretesting procedures and when one wishes

to gain a quick insight into a social phenomenon.

Quota Sampling

In quota sampling the researcher selects some people from each sector of the population. For example, in studying the views of university students towards a particular issue, the researcher with a general knowledge about the characteristics of the students may decide to obtain views from a group of students from each Hall. He includes some of the people on the basis of their social and demographic characteristics. The elements are taken according to the proportion in which the sampler thinks they appear in the population. The critical requirement is that there should be enough cases from each segment of the population to make possible an estimation of the population-stratum value. Basically, it remains non-probabilistic in the sense that the sampling estimation and selection procedures are determined in a practical manner. It is, therefore, difficult for the sampler to calculate meaningfully the extent and nature of error inherent in the sample estimates.

In pilot studies, the researcher may wish to gain a quick insight into the nuances of his research problem. He may wish to pretest his questionnaire design. He may also wish to generate some hypotheses from the field situation. In such cases, he goes to the field to select various groups of people he thinks can answer his research questions and may resort to taking quotas from each identified group.

Chapter 3

METHODS OF DATA COLLECTION

INTRODUCTION

In social research, we collect data from the social world. The researcher develops field strategies to enable him to find answers to research questions. To get answers to his questions, he must go to the field. In a household survey, for example, his strategy may be to use a questionnaire for his respondents to answer. The respondents are the people he selects to interview to get answers to his research questions. It was in this connection that in the previous chapter, we dealt with the problems and issues of sampling. It was pointed out that sampling procedures can enable us to get to the specific operational world and to find our respondents. After the sampling selection, the researcher starts his fieldwork.

Many methods are used in social research to collect data. It is, however, important to note that the selection of a particular method to collect data must be decided upon in the light of one's problem. In making this decision, the researcher must keep in mind the type of people he is dealing with, the nature of the social situation, the mood of the social environment and the psychology of the people. It is also necessary to use more than one method to collect data. Using various suitable methods to collect data will help the researcher to evaluate his data source and to detect inconsistent answers.

The commonly-used methods are questionnaire, interviewing, direct observation, participant observation, case studies, life history, the use of documentary evidence, letters, personal memoranda, diaries, public records, panel discussion and group discussions. The important point is to use an appropriate method or methods to collect data in a particular situation. Blumer (1970: 20) argues that "there is no protocol to be followed in the use of any one of these procedures; the procedure should be adapted to its circumstances and guided by judgment of its propriety and fruitfulness. One should sedulously seek participants in the sphere of life who are acute observers and who are well informed".

The scientist must know that field; he must learn to establish rapport, and he must develop insightful strategy in selecting an appropriate method in order to collect reliable and valid data. If he chooses to use informants, he must come to that decision judiciously. The informants must be trained to get an insight into the research objectives and must be able to gain access to information. Again, as Blumer remarks: "a small number of such individuals brought together as a discussion and resource group, is more valuable many times over than any representative sample. Such a group, discussing collectively their sphere of life and probing into it as they meet one another's disagreements, will do more to lift the veils covering the sphere of life than any other device that we know of" (Blumer 1970: 33). The investigator must check the background of his informants. This must be done in the field so that if there are any inconsistencies they can be detached and corrected.

Five frequently used methods of social research are discussed presently.

PARTICIPANT OBSERVATION

It is a method of data collection whereby the field worker goes to live and to participate in the daily activities of the people he is studying. He gets to know his respondents. From that point, he starts to observe the situation in order to find answers to his research questions. He participates in some of the activities of the people which will allow him to get a relevant insight into his problem. He needs to be acquainted with the people and to acquire a position in the setting. After getting to understand the matrix of the social setting, he begins to collect data. Studies which employ the method of participant observation involve repeated genuine social relationship and interaction with the social actors in the scene of activities. The research worker becomes part of the situation and part of the data-gathering process. This method gives him an inside look.

In entering the field, the researcher introduces himself properly to the local authorities, to the chief of the area, to the prominent people, to informal leaders and to members of the local development committee, so as to gain a legitimate entry into their community. It may be necessary for him to inform the leaders about the aim of his project. His stated objectives must be made clear. If these are not clarified, the community leaders and opinion setters may tend to be suspicious of him as an "intruder". Sometimes it may be assumed that such a person has been sent to them to spy on their activities, and/or to collect material on which their tax assessment will be based. The field worker must foresee these difficulties in order to adopt appropriate field strategies to help him to gain legitimate entry into the field. He needs to establish a rapport with the members of the community. The establishment of a field rapport means that the field worker must learn to get on well with his respondents. He must learn their ways, understand their culture, fears and expectations in order to fit into their setting.

In many Ghanaian communities, we are usually dealing with a rural and traditional people. Most of them are illiterates. For example in Ghana, about 71 per cent of the people live in rural and outlying areas. They share a rural cosmology. They live in a village social setting based on respect for the elders. These rural areas and small towns are kinship-based societies. The social organization of these areas is quite different from that of the urban areas of Ghana. Relatives may not necessarily live in the same geographical area. Children may stay with their mothers in other households in a separate house; at night a wife may join her husband or the children may come to eat with their fathers or uncles. These factors and other prevailing social norms must be taken into account in fieldwork. The researcher needs some ingenuity to understand a household unit in a typical rural Ghanaian settlement. It is not easy to define even a household unit.

Important household decisions may be taken collectively, by various kin groups; so the fieldworker must be extremely careful to locate the actual heads of households to determine opinion leaders. He needs also to know the decision-makers, the prime movers of social action in order to understand the nature of their household relationship. These problems of fieldwork can be overcome if the local social organization is properly understood. He must learn the language or employ field assistants who can speak the local language.

After these important preliminaries, he begins data collection by participating in the daily life of the group. He watches the people he is studying to see what situations are typical, what patterns develop, who interacts with whom, who initiates important decisions and how the people behave. He may enter into daily informal conversations with some of the people to discover the meanings of their social acts and the interpretations they assign to them. For example, if he is studying funerals and their social significance, he attends various funerals, participates in the activities, talks with different types of mourners, seeks to find the manifest and the latent functions of the funeral celebration. He must get to the meaning of the funeral celebration in the particular social setting. He must look at the participants, he must record their crucial activities, study the types of people, their background and other social characteristics. He studies the setting, the norms of behaviour and the specific purpose of the various types of people at the gathering. These approaches to observation will give him an insight into the social arena. The observer may want to know the relationship between the participants. How are they related to one another and to the situation under investigation? How many are present? He may also want to know the background characteristics of the people: age, sex, migratory status of the people, their educational, occupational, religious and kinship backgrounds. He raises questions as to what kinds of behaviour the situation encourages, permits or discourages; what goals other than the manifest purpose the people seem to be pursuing; and considers whether the aims of the various groups of people related are compatible or incompatible. These questions if pursued diligently will help him to understand what really goes on in the situation.

If he is from a different social background, he needs to be careful not to impose his own values and social orientation on the new social situation. Many of the research assistants are usually recruited from the university students population. The point to be remembered in this regard is that the observer is in a relatively different social position when he goes to the field. He must not act in any way that might suggest that he looks down upon the people he is observing. He must in all humility learn to accept the social environment in which he finds himself. The observer needs to record what he sees in terms of its intensity, persistency, unusualness, its duration and its effects in a freely objective manner. Personal biases must be kept out.

In research situations, the participant observer is confronted with the problem of note-taking in recording his observation. He must assess the nuances of the responses. Regarding the appropriateness of taking notes or recording any kind of information, a word of caution is necessary here. Speaking from field experience of rural people, it is not always appropriate to pull out a piece of paper and a pencil to start recording. The flow of the conversation will be interrupted; an artificial social environment will be created and sometimes the people will begin to grow suspicious about the activities of the observer. For these reasons, the researcher must take a mental picture of what goes on to enable him to record his observation as soon as he leaves the observational scene. At the end of the day's activities when the fieldworker retires to his room, he begins to write his notes. It is at this place that he begins to record the important happenings.

An interesting aspect of the role of the participant observer is that he will get the opportunity to check his data in the field. He can go back to the field in order to verify what has escaped him. For this reason, it is appropriate to make it a habit to record the daily activities. It must also be pointed out that the technique of participant observation is in fact a combination of two methods, interviewing (which is informal) and a direct observation. The crucial point is that the interviewer must be shrewd enough to see what is going on. He must raise relevant and sensitive questions at appropriate times and must sense the psychology of the people to know when to introduce sensitive questions and when to vary his style of doing things.

Opponents of the participant observation technique argue that the method is too loose and that the data are not quantifiable. The argument goes on to say that there is an observer's bias and that there are personal and subjective infusion of ideas so that it becomes difficult to disentangle the truth from the opinion. It is argued further that the observer can lower his sense of objectivity in the process of "going native" so to speak. These criticisms can be overcome if the observer adopts the following strategy: he must (1) outline his objective (2) bear his specific questions in mind and (3) use both qualitative and quantitative data to get some understanding of the social phenomena. For example, at a funeral celebration, he must observe the behaviour of the people by noting the number of people present, what specific acts are performed and ask for the reasons for their acts. In these instances, the observer would be able to get specific information before he looks for particular issues and indicators which will help him to answer his research questions. He must check his data sources in order to detect errors. These measures will given him a critical approach.

In such field studies, the researcher needs some help from informants and research assistants. He cannot do it alone. The fieldworkers must be selected carefully. In finding field assistants, one must consider the following: their interest in research work, their technical skills in the field, their ability to carry out field research under trying rural conditions, their honesty of purpose, adaptability to field situations, knowledge of the local language and their understanding of the norms of the community.

The usual practice, after the logistics of the particular research project has been determined, is to advertise the project in the daily media and on college and university notice boards for the recruitment of field assistants. In the universities, students are encouraged to work on research projects to gain research insights and to earn extra money during the long vacation (July–September). The good ones must be selected and trained to acquaint them with the sensitivities of field work. The training is necessary to enable the assistants know what the research is about and in providing them with the necessary research background. They are trained to check the source of data and to ask meaningful questions by probing. After the training period, they are distributed to the various communities where their expertise is needed. That is to say, each field assistant must be specifically selected and given a place to work on the basis of his special background and level of competence. It cannot be over-emphasized that the bulk of data collection, in this day and age, depends on the quality of the field assistants; therefore, they must be properly selected, trained, remunerated and oriented to the study's objectives. Training can help them to improve the reliability and validity of data collected by them.

In the field of operation, additional knowledgeable informants must be recruited to assist in collecting data. Again, the informants must be properly selected, trained, and oriented to the aims of the study. Usually, the informants are recruited from the community on the basis of their knowledge of community affairs, and their acceptability to the members of the community. The data collected by them must, however, be checked constantly to iron out inconsistencies.

As a method, participant observation is a useful one in the collection of field data. In the rural social setting, where the majority of the people cannot read and write, this method is a suitable one.

INTERVIEWS

It is a method of field investigation whereby the researcher meets his respondents and through the interaction he asks specific questions to find answers to his research problem. This method is used when respondents are willing to talk and have knowledge of the research problem. The researcher prepares an interview schedule consisting of several specific questions, or various aspects of the topic under investigation. Then during his encounter with the respondents, he asks specific questions. Some questions may also emerge from the field discussion. These are usually unstructured.

The interviewing technique is an appropriate method for all segments of the population. The only point is that the interviewer must speak the language of the people and must be able to communicate with the various people he meets. It presupposes an understanding of the culture of the local people and the ability to establish a rapport. Interviewing offers flexibility. This is because the interviewer is in a position to sense the situation and can adapt his questions to suit the psychology of the people involved in the field situation. The interviewing situation creates a learning environment in which the two, the researcher and the respondent, are involved in a purposeful discussion. Many people find the interviewing technique to be non-threatening. Intensive field training is necessary to produce a good interview. We find the interviewing method a suitable device in collecting data from rural and illiterate people. The interviewer can asses the mood of the people and can appraise the validity and reliability of the answers. The interviewer is also in a unique position to check his data and to observe what is actually going on. He probes any contradictory information with certain types of research topics such as those which deal with value-oriented questions. The interviewing method is a useful one. Questions are asked, feedback is provided and within a relaxed atmosphere, information is sought and checked. The interviewer can watch "sensibly" the sentiments that may accompany the answers. He can appropriately vary the tone of his conversation to fit into the prevailing social atmosphere.

Sometimes, the interviewer may be tempted to inject a bit of his own feelings into the situation. This must be avoided. The interviewer should not use his own preconceptions to interpret the information he gets from the field. He must remain objective. He must follow specific instructions, express himself fully. We must guard against the situation in which the interviewer chooses only his friends to interview. They may not know much about the problem under discussion. This type of problem occurs quite commonly in situations where there is a lack of effective supervision. The interviewer may grow tired so he settles in to interview people who happen to be around but have no knowledge about the problem. We must guard against this source of error by choosing the appropriate field assistants and by providing them with effective supervisory to ensure adherent to only the sample selected. The interviewing technique if used judiciously can be a useful addition to participant observation. The researcher must give his field assistants instruction, the pros and cons of the method, the value of the research, and the value of rechecking field information.

There is a basic interrelationship between the Questionnaire and interview methods. The interview method is an alternative method of collecting survey data. Rather than asking people to answer formal written down questions and enter their own answers, field researcher may send interviewers to ask questions orally in the field around a research topic and objectives then the answers are recorded and other emerging issues may be clarified from the field situation. It is usually done in a face to face encounter.

The interviewers should be properly trained and schooled in the subject matter and in the specific objectives of the research work in order to avoid biases and field errors.

In some field situations, a combination of the two methods may be used. That is a questionnaire is formally prepared and an interviewer is employed to administer the questionnaire. This is often called an interview schedule. There is a higher level of response rate than if the questionnaire is left to the person, the respondent, to answer in his or her own free time. The presence of the interviewer is important in increasing the total response rate. Respondents seem more reluctant to turn down an interviewer who is standing by the doorstep than they are to throw away a questionnaire which is sent or posted to them. The following is an illustrative interview schedule. This has both pre-coded and open-ended questions and interviews were conducted in rural communities.

UNIVERSITY OF CAPE COAST*
DEPARTMENT OF SOCIOLOGY
SD/MSC/RCS/1990/HQ ....

HOUSEHOLD INTERVIEW SCHEDULE ON:

THE ROLE OF RURAL CREDIT IN AGRICULTURAL AND RURAL DEVEL-
OPMENT IN GHANA: THE CASE OF THE KETA DISTRICT

INTRODUCTION

This is a study being conducted by the Department of Sociology, University of Cape Coast to find out whether there is a relationship between rural credit and rural development. We therefore appeal to you to answer the following questions as candidly as possible.

Thank you in advance for your cooperation.

Instructions

1.   Where alternatives have been provided ring the code number only.
2.   For other questions write your answer in the space provided.

SECTION 1
DEMOGRAPHIC DATA

1.   List all members of the household in relations to the head of household.

Relationship to	Sex		Age (Yrs)
	M	F	
1. Head of household			
2.			
3.			
4.			
5.			
6.			
7.			
8.			
9.			
10.			

---

* Culled from Ganu, K. M. (1991). *The Role of Rural Credit in Agricultural and Rural Development in Ghana: The Case of the Keta District.* Unpublished MSc Thesis, Faculty of Social Sciences, University of Cape Coast. Published by kind permission of the author and the Faculty of Social Sciences, University of Cape Coast, Cape Coast.

No. in household (For office use only) ....

2.   Sex of respondent: 1. Male   2. Female

3.   Age of Respondent (last Birthday)

4.   Place of Origin

    1. From the locality   4. Other region
    2. Other place in the district   5. Non-Ghanaian
    3. Another district in the region.

5.   If immigrant, do you come from a: 1. Rural area   2. Urban area

6.   Marital Status: Are you now

    1. Single   3. Divorced   5. Separated
    2. Married   4. Widowed

7.   If married (male) how many wives do you have?

8.   If not single, how many children do you have?

9.   What is the highest level of literacy you attained?

    1. Never   8. Teacher Training College
    2. Adult literacy class   9. Polytechnic
    3. Primary School   10. Secondary Form 6
    4. Middle School/JSS   11. Specialist College
    5. Secondary Form 5   12. University
    6. Commercial/Vocational   13. Other, specify
    7. Technical

10. How many children/dependants of school-going age do you have now in:

    1. No formal education   7. Teacher Training College
    2. Primary   8. Polytechnic
    3. Middle Form 4   9. Secondary Form 6
    4. Junior Secondary School   10. Specialist College
    5. Secondary/Commercial   11. University
    6. Technical/Vocational

SECTION II
ACCOMMODATION

11. Type of house:

    1. Raffia/"kloba" hut with thatch roof
    2. Raffia/"kloba" hut with zinc roof
    3. Mud house with thatch roof
    4. Mud house with zinc roof
    5. Cement block house with thatch roof
    6. Cement block house with zinc roof
    7. Other, specify ....

12. Is the house you are living in your

    1. Own house   5. Mother's house
    2. Wife's house   6. Relative's house
    3. Husband's house   7. Rented house
    4. Father's house   8. Government's house

13. How many bedrooms do you have in the house?

14. Which of the following facilities exist in the house?

    1. Sitting/Living Room   4. Toilet/latrine
    2. Kitchen   5. Water (well/pipe borne)
    3. Bathroom

15. If you do not have the following facilities in the house, indicate where
    you usually get them

Facility	where obtained
1. Kitchen 2. Water (well/pipe-borne) 3. Toilet/Latrine 4. Bathroom	

16. Which of the following facilities do your children/dependants in school
    have access to?

    1. Their own rooms   3. Electric light/lantern
    2. Tables and chairs

17. Do you find your present accommodation adequate?

    1. Not adequate   3. Adequate
    2. Fairly adequate   4. Very adequate

18. If not adequate, what are you doing about it?
    1. Nothing   4. Looking for bigger house to rent
    2. Making extension   5. Other, specify
    3. Building new house

19. Do you have another house(s) elsewhere?

    1. None   4.   In another district in the region
    2. In the locality   5.   In another region
    3. In this district

SECTION III
EMPLOYMENT AND INCOME

A. **Employment**

20. Do you do or have you done any work which has given you some income since 1988?

Year	Yes	No	If No, why
1988			
1989			
1990			

21. Are you now

    1. Self-employed?   2. Working for someone?
    or 3. Both self-employed and working for someone?

22. What is your main (primary) occupation?

    1. Farming   7. Petty-trading
    2. Fishing   8. Civil servant
    3. Foodstuff marketing   9. Teaching
    4. Fish processing/marketing 10. Para-medical staff
    5. Handicrafts work   11. (Farm) labourer
    6. Artisan (e.g. mason)   12. Other, specify ....

23. List three other occupations you engage in for which you earn some income, in order of importance of income derived.

    1.   2.   3.

24. If self-employed (Q21), do you employ other people to work for you/ and on what basis?

    1. Do not employ   3. Employ permanent workers
    2. Employ casual workers   4. Employ contract workers

25. How many people did you employ in 1989 and how many have you employed for work in 1990?

Type	No employed	
	1989	1990
Permanent workers Contract workers Causal workers		

26. How do you pay your workers/and how much?

Type of worker	Nature of Payment	
	Cash	Produce/kind
Permanent Contract Casual		

27. Can you indicate members of your household who assist you in your work?

    1. Spouse   4. Sisters   6. Nieces
    2. Children   5. Nephews   7. Other, specify
    3. Brothers

B. **Income**

28. How much did you earn from your various occupations in 1990 and 1989?

Occupation	Income	
	1990 (¢)	1989 (¢)
1. 2. 3. 4.		

29. Do you find the income you receive from all occupations adequate?

   1. Yes   2. No.

30. If No, what are you doing or would you want to do to improve the situation?

31. Do you think the wages and prices you receive for your produce represent a fair return to your efforts?

   1. Yes   2. No.

32. If No, why?

C.   Production Assets and Inputs

33. List all fixed production assets and equipment you have or use in your occupations in order of importance (e.g. land, canoe).

Item	Size/Quantity	Cost/Unit
1. 2. 3. 4. 5. 6.		

34. How were these acquired? Name two ways only.

   1. Inherited   3. Bought from loans
   2. Bought from own resources   4. Hired
   5. Other, specify

35. List all variable inputs (e.g. manure, fuel) used in your occupation(s) in order of importance.

Item	Cost/Unit
1.	
2.	
3.	
4.	
5	

36. Where do you usually obtain your inputs?

    1. In the locality   4. In Accra
    2. In the nearest big town 5. Other specify
    3. At Keta

37. Are these production assets and inputs readily available?
    1. Yes   2. No

38. If No, why are they not?

    1.
    2.
    3.

39. Do you think the prices of production assets and inputs are high or low?
    1. High   2. Low.

40. If high, suggest measures to bring down prices.

    1.   2.

41. Do some members of your community have greater access to production assets and inputs and who?

    1. No   5.   Small farmers
    2. Big farmers   6. Small fishermen
    3. Big fishermen   7.   Other, specify
    4. The educated

D. **Agricultural Services and Cooperatives**

42. Do you know of the Farmers' Services Company?
    1. Yes   2. No

43.   Have you ever obtained any service or input from the Farmers Services
      Company? State nature of service.

Response	Type of Service/why not?
1. Yes 2. No	

44.   Have you ever obtained any service or inputs from the Extension Services
      Division of the Ministry of Agriculture? State nature of service/why not?

Response	Type of Service/Why not?
1. Yes 2. No	

45.   Do you think the Extension Services Division is doing enough to improve
      agriculture production? How or Why?

      Response   How/Why

      1. Yes
      2. No
      3. DK

46.   Do you belong to any cooperative society? Yes   No.

47.   If, No, why?

48.   If Yes, which one?

49.   What benefits do you derive from your membership?

      1.
      2.
      3.

SECTION IV
SOURCES OF CREDIT AND CREDIT USE

50.   Have you ever borrowed money?   1. Yes   2. No

51. If No, why?

52. If yes, who usually gives you the loan? Name all sources.

    1. Friends
    2. Relatives
    3. Traders
    4. Customers
    5. Money lenders
    6. Cooperative Credit Union
    7. Bank
    8. Other, specify

53. Why did you take the loan(s)? (Give all reasons)

    Consumption

    1. Buy food
    2. Buy clothing
    3. Pay educational bills
    4. Perform marriage
    5. Perform religious rites
    6. Pay funeral expenses
    7. Rebuild/repair house

    Production

    8. Pay medical bills
    9. Buy/hire farmland
    10. Buy/hire fishing gear
    11. Buy implements (e.g. hoe)
    12. Buy inputs (e.g. fertilizer)
    13. Pay workers/labourers
    14. Other, specify

54. How much loan did you take from each of the following sources since 1988?

Source	1990	1989	1988
1. Friends			
2. Relatives			
3. Trader			
4. Customers			
5. Money lenders			
6. Cooperative Credit Union			
7. Other, specify			

55. Which of the sources of credit do you prefer and why?

Source	Reasons for Preference
1. Friends	
2. Relatives	
3. Traders	
4. Customers	
5. Money lenders	
6. Cooperative Credit Union	
7. Bank	
8. Other, specify	

56.   In what form do you prefer loan and why? Cash or commodity loan.

Type of Loan	Reason for Preference
1. Cash 2. Commodity/Inputs 3. Indifferent	

B.   **Access to Credit**

57.   Which of the sources of credit do you consider more accessible?

1. Institutional sources

2. Non-institutional

58.   State two reasons why you consider the one source more accessible and the other less accessible.

More Accessible	Less Accessible
1. 2.	

59.   Do you think some members of your community have greater   access to credit?

1. Yes   2. No

60.   If Yes, who and why do you think so?

Category	Reason
1. Big farmers/fishermen 2. Small farmers/fishermen 3. Market women/traders 4. The educated 5. Illiterates 6. Businessmen 7. Artisans 8. Other, specify	

61.   What main problems do you consider as hampering rural credit delivery? (Give all reasons)

1. Lack of banks
2. High Interest rates
3. Lack of collaterals
4. High risk in agriculture

5. Unwillingness to repay
6. Loan diversion
7. Lack of banking education
8. Other, specify

C. **Terms of Credit**

62. What conditions were attached to the loans you took?

Conditions	1990	1989	1988
1. No condition 2. Interest payment 3. Collateral security 4. Profit sharing 5. Purchase of produce/catch 6. Other, specify			

63. If you provided security, state nature of the security

1. Production assets (e.g. farmland)
2. Economic trees
3. Creeks

4. Jewels/clothes
5. House
6. Other, specify

64. How much interest did you pay or are you expected to pay on the loans you took from all sources?

Source	Interest (Amount/percentage)		
	1990	1989	1988
1. Friends 2. Relatives 3. Traders 4. Customers 5. Money lenders 6. Cooperative Credit Union 7. Bank 8. Other, specify			

65. Would you consider the interest high or low?

1. High   2. Low

66. Indicate the average period of repayment for the loans you took and state whether adequate or inadequate?

Source	Period	Adequate	Inadequate
1. Banks 2. Other sources			

67. Were you able to repay each loan you took out

Year	Yes	Still paying	No
1990 1989 1988			

68. If No., why? ....

69. If still paying, how much do you have overdue for payment for the loans you took out

Year	Amount Overdue (¢)
1990 1989 1988	

70. Are you deprived of any pledged property due to default on loan repayment?   1. Yes   2. No

71. If Yes, state how this has affected your work and output.

    1.
    2.
    3.

D. **Credit and Agricultural Development**

72. If you took loan(s) for production did you use it for that?
    1. Yes   2. No

73. If No, why did you not? ....

74. If Yes, has the loan improved your production capacity and how?

    1. No improvement
    2. Larger farmland
    3. Better farm implements
    4. More irrigation wells
    5. Bought more seeds (e.g. shallot)
    6. Bought new nets
    7. Bought new canoe
    8. Bought an outboard motor
    9. Built more fish smoking kilns
    10. Other, specify

75. Did you employ more people to work for you as a result of the loan(s) you took and how many?

Type of worker	1990	1989
1. None		
2. Permanent		
3. Contract		
4. Casual		

76. Did your output/income increase as a result of the loan you took?

    1. Yes   2. No

77. How did you use the increased income you had?

    1. Buy more food
    2. Buy more clothings
    3. Repair/rebuilt house
    4. Build a new house
    5. Settle educational bills
    6. Acquire more production assets
    7. Buy more production inputs
    8. Settle overdue debts
    9. Buy a vehicle for my work
    10. Buy a vehicle for private use
    11. Other, specify

78. Is your life made better or worse off by the loans(s) you took and how?

Response	How
1. Better off 2. Worse off 3. The same	

79. Would you want to take any loans in the future and for what?

Response	Purpose
1. Yes 2. No	

E.   Savings

80. Do you save money?   1. Yes   2. No

81. If yes, where do you save? ....

   1. *Esɔ* (*Susu*) Group   4. Bank
   2. Credit Union   5. Self
   3. Life Insurance   6. Other, specify

82. What benefit can one get from saving? (Name two benefits).

   1. No benefit   4. Easier access to credit
   2. Interest paid   5. Other, specify
   3. Provide for emergency

83. If no savings, why not? ....

SECTION V
CREDIT AND RURAL DEVELOPMENT

84. For each of the following facilities/amenities, state whether the community has it, needs it and who provided it?

Item	Have	Need	Provided by
1. Public toilet/latrine 2. Public well water 3. Pipe-borne water			

4. Good roads			
5. Electricity supply			
6. Hospital/health centre			
7. Primary school			
8. Junior Secondary School			
9. Second-cycle school			
10. Police station			
11. Agriculture Extension Office			
12. Banks			
13. Transport services			
14. Tractor hiring service			
15. Agriculture Inputs Supply Depot			
16. Community Centre			
17. Football Park			
18. Market			
19. Post Office			

85. Do you find the facilities the community has adequate or inadequate?

Code	Facility	Adequate	Inadequate

86. For each of the amenities you think the community needs (Question 82), state whether it is very important, important or not important to make life worth living.

Code	Facility	Very Important	Important	Not Important

87. Who do you think should provide these amenities?

1. Central Government   3. The Community
2. District Assembly   4. Other, specify

88. If the community decides to provide these amenities, what contribu-

tion would you make and how much or how often?

Contribution	Amount/How often
1. Free labour 2. Cash (money) 3. Building materials 4. Other, specify	

89. Which of the amenities do you have in your house (Q.14) were provided as a result of the improvement in your production/catch?

    1. Water (well/pipe-borne)   4. Bathroom
    2. Toilet/latrine   5. None
    3. Light (electricity/lantern)

90. If your income increased or if you produce more would you contribute more towards the improvement of your community?

    1. Yes   2. No

91. If No, why not?

92. If you were to contribute money or materials towards the improvement of your community what three items in order of priority would you want to have?

    1.
    2.
    3.

93. Do you know or have you heard about rural banks?

    1. Yes   2. No

94. What benefits do you think rural people can get from rural banks?

    1. No benefits   5. Provide commodity loans
    2. Provide facility for saving 6. Longer payment period for loan
    3. Provide finance for   7. Demand collaterals that rural
       agriculture   people can offer
    4. Help rural development   8. Other, specify

95. If your community decides to set up a rural bank, would you buy shares in it?   1. Yes   2. No

96. If no, why not?

97. Do you think the average rural dweller is adequately protected by Government aid against natural disasters?   1. Yes   2. No

98. If Yes, what kind of protection? (Give all kinds)

    1. Provision of building materials
    2. Resettlement of affected persons
    3. Supply of agricultural inputs to affected persons
    4. Provision of loans to affected persons to buy fresh inputs
    5. Supply of relief food items
    6. Supply of relief clothing/bankers
    7. Other, specify

99. If No, what kind of protection would you want the government to provide?

    1.
    2.
    3.
    4.

Appreciation
It has been very nice talking to you. Thank you for sparing so much of your time in the interest of rural development.

To be completed by the interviewer

1. Name of interviewer
2. Date and time interview started
3. Date and time interview completed

4. Locality
5. House No.
6. No of households in the house

Interviewer's Remarks: ....

....

....

....

....

QUESTIONNAIRE

Formal questions can be framed and written down for the respondents to provide the answers. As a method for data collection, the questionnaire is an efficient way to collect statistically quantifiable information. It is an efficient method in the sense that many respondents can be reached within a short space of time. But whether it helps the investigator to collect reliable data is an open question.

In constructing a questionnaire, the field problems must be outlined and the objectives specified. Each objective should give the researcher a clear focus in order to formulate relevant questions. They must be clearly stated and functionally specific. The language must be clear; ambiguity must be avoided. The questions must be framed in a socially-acceptable way. Some of the questions may be framed in a pre-coded format or in an open-ended form.

Pre-coded Questionnaire

In a pre-coded form of questionnaire construction, the investigator sets questions, and at the same time, provides all the possible answers he expects to obtain from his respondents. In this way, it is easy for his respondents to respond to the appropriate answer.

The following are examples of the pre-coded types of questionnaire construction:

1. Age . . .
   1. 15 – 79
   2. 20 – 24
   3. 25 – 29
   4. 30 – 34
   5. 35 – 39
   6. 40 +

2. Sex . . .
   1. Male
   2. Female

3. Place of Birth
   1. Rural
   2. Urban

4. Usual Place of Residence
   1. Rural
   2. Urban

5. Secondary School attended
   1. Achimota
   2. Mfantsipim
   3. Wesley Girls
   4. Adisadel
   5. Accra Academy
   6. Holy Child
   7. Other — specify

6. Religion
   1. Catholic
   2. Moslem
   3. Presbyterian
   4. Methodist
   5. Other — specify

7. Education of Parents
   1. Literate
   2. Illiterate

These questions are examples of pre-coded type of questions on background information. Usually, the researcher may not be in a position to know all the possible responses; in that case he must leave enough room for his respondents to give additional information by stating "Other (specify)" or "any other comments". The interviewee is expected to tick ( ) or ring O the code number of the appropriate response. They have a built-in-time-saving device. In this case, the respondent is called upon to select the responses which reflect his true position. The pre-coded form of questions is an efficient method in the collection of data from literate population. It facilitates coding. However, it must be noted that certain types of questions are difficult to frame in pre-coded form. So in normal questionnaire schedule, we must use both the pre-coded and the open-ended questions.

Open-ended Questions

The open-ended types of questions are framed as specific questions with no possible answers provided. The investigator writes down the questions and he expects his respondents to give their own answers. Open-ended questions give flexibility in answering questions. Respondents can express themselves as fully as they wish. It means, however, that the respondent must think about his own frame of answers. Because of the varied nature of the answers, their processing is time consuming. It takes a lot of time to construct the coding frame and to code open-ended questions.

Examples of open-ended type of questions are:

1.   How do you store your drinking water? ....

....

2.   Why did you decide to come to hospital? ....

....

3.   What are some of your aspirations? ....

....

In framing questions, we must think not only of designing questions that are easy to answer but also how to get valid data. For this reasons, both the open-ended and pre-coded types of questions must be used judiciously. In the area of attitudes, values and beliefs, it is better to use open-ended questions. This gives the respondents enough room for self-expression.

The following is an example of a completed questionnaire schedule (which includes an introductory statement and the main questions). It was designed to help evaluate courses at the Department of Sociology. The respondents were undergraduate students of the department.

As a general guide, when one starts to design a questionnaire or an interview schedule one must raise these points. Are the questions necessary? Do they help to answer the research problem? Do the people have the information needed on the subject? Will the respondents be able to give the necessary information? Are the questions clear and distinct? Will they be misunderstood? Have we avoided ambiguities or unclear concepts? Great skill goes into the construction of a questionnaire. The questions must be free from spurious relationship and from vagueness. It is always advisable to consult other specialists to read the questions and to help to make corrections. No social survey can be better than its questions. Expert approach and guidance are important components in questionnaire construction. After the preliminaries, the researcher must pre-test his questions. The pre-test is a try-out test for the validity of the questions, for examining how meaningful they are and for determining whether there is any need to change or modify or include certain questions before the actual fieldwork is undertaken. The pre-test serves as a means to detect and to solve unforeseen difficulties in the wording and placement of the questions. The final questionnaire is then subjected to editorial work by examining its content, its form, arrangement, logical sequence, meaning and style of wording.

Additional Questionnaire

Let us give an example of pre-coded and open-ended types of questionnaire construction. In designing questions for a district assembly evaluation in rural areas. Firstly, there is the need to provide a background information, then the main questions may follow this trend; knowledge, attitudes and practice types.

A. Background of Respondents

1. Age
    1. 15–19
    2. 20–24
    3. 25–29
    4. 30–34
    5. 35–39
    6. 40–44
    7. 45–49
    8. 50–54
    9. 55–59
    10. 60–64
    11. 65–69
    12. 70– +

2. Sex
    1. Male
    2. Female

3. Place of Birth
    1. Rural
    2. Urban

4. If rural specify   Village ....

5.   If urban specify   Town   ....

6.   Usual place of residence   1. Rural
                                    2. Urban

7.   Are you formally employed   1. Yes 2. No

8.   If yes, occupation   1. Farmer
                                    2. Fishfolk
                                    3. Artisan (specify)
                                    4. Clerical (specify)
                                    5. Trader
                                    6. Other (specify)

9.   Religion   1. Christian
                                    2. Moslem
                                    3. Other (specify)

10.   If Christian, specify denomination ....

11.   Education   1. No Formal School
                                    2. Formal Schooling

12.   If Formal Schooling specify   1. Up to Elementary School
                                    2. Up to Secondary School
                                    3. Up to Teacher Training
                                    4. Commercial
                                    5. University
                                    6. Others, Specify

13.   Marital Status   1. Not Married
                                    2. Single
                                    3. Married
                                    4. Other Specify ....

B.   Knowledge Types

1.   What is the name of the district? ....

2.   Main occupation of inhabitants? ....

3. Type of schools? ....

4. Any hospitals or clinics?   1. Yes   2. No

5. Is there electricity supply?   1. Yes   2. No

6. Type of water supply?   1. Pipe-borne
                               2. Boreholes
                               3. Stream/River
                               4. Other specify ....

7. Road Network   1. Tarred
                               2. Untarred

8. Main farm produce (specify) ....

9. Do you know your assembly members?   1. Yes 2. No

C. Attitude

1. What is your attitude towards the
    district assembly: 1. Favourable
                               2. Unfavourable

2. If favourable specify the reason..
    ....
    ....

3. If not favourable specify the reason ....
    ....
    ....

4. What is your attitude towards the
    District Chief Executive?   1. Favourable
                                   2. Unfavourable

5. If favourable specify ....

....

....

6.   If not favourable specify ....

....

D.   Practice

1.   What role do you play to make the district function (effective)?

2.   Did you vote at the last district elections? 1. Yes   2. No

3.   If no, why did you not vote? ....

....

4.   What can be done to upgrade the effectiveness of the district? (please be specific)

....

....

5.   Provide any further comments ....

....

Thank you.

Questionnaire and Non-literate Population

Is the questionnaire method an appropriate technique for studying a non-literate population? In the Ghanaian situation, many research workers use the questionnaire method and they frame questions in English. The population is significantly rural and non-literate. Many of the people hardly speak or write English. The illiterates speak various Ghanaian languages, mainly Akan, Ewe, Ga and Dagbani. For this reason, the serious research scientist must of necessity translate his questions into the local language, especially the leading concepts before he starts his fieldwork. His research assistants must be selected on the basis of their understanding of the local languages in the study areas. Otherwise, there will be a communication block and the questionnaire method would be ineffective.

Even in the urban Ghanaian situation, many of the people can only speak superficial English. The researcher must not be complacent in the knowledge that because they are literate they can communicate effectively with them in English. Many of the people have only a shallow understanding of English words and phrases. The researcher, therefore, must be aware of some of these local difficulties. For example, in carrying out a field research in Achimota Village, a suburb in Accra, the author experienced some of these difficulties. The respondents were asked whether they had "toilet facilities" in their houses. The reply was no in almost all the houses. It was detected then that the word "toilet' might not have been properly understood. So the next day, the fieldworkers were asked to go to the same households and to ask the respondents if they had "latrine" in their houses. This word was understood by them and they responded generally in the affirmative. The point of emphasis is that we could have avoided this error if we had studied the terms commonly used in the community.

Problems in Using Questionnaire

In dealing with an illiterate population, the fieldworkers must not put words in the mouth of the respondents. They must be careful not to suggest a particular answer. They must be given daily supervision to encourage the fieldworkers to do an honest day's work to reflect what actually happened in the field. The usual field complaints are boredom, difficulty in getting respondents to answer questions, lack of time, inability to meet respondents and difficulties in explaining concepts.

It is difficult to overcome some of these problems. Nevertheless, we need to take notice of them in order to find appropriate ways and means to structure questions which will be meaningful and less time-consuming, especially when we deal with rural people. Furthermore, in entering the field, there is the need for the fieldworker to find suitable times he can meet people. We need to know the times rural respondents are usually available and willing to answer questions. These measures will assist the fieldworker to cut down the non-response rate.

Reliability and Validity

To increase the level of reliability and validity of measurement, the researcher must include questions which can help him to detect errors. For example, if the question "Would you like to live next door to a particular religious group?" is put and the answer is no, then we expect "no" to the next question: "Would you like to marry from this particular religious group?" If the answer is "yes", then we can detect clearly, all things being equal, that there is misunderstanding somewhere, so there is need to check. Such questions should be introduced to detect errors. Fieldworkers must be trained to detect such errors and to correct them.

We must guard against the problem whereby fieldworkers begin to be unreliable by answering the questions themselves. They must be selected on the basis of their prior experience, seriousness, industry, honesty of purpose in research studies. In addition, they must be given constant field supervision and proper incentives.

The questionnaire method must be used with care. The researcher must think seriously about his topic and decide whether questionnaire is an appropriate method. He must think about the nature of the social structure he is dealing with. In traditional settings, where the public is largely illiterate, sensitive questions must be introduced with care. Non-literate people tend to live in groups among their relatives. Embarrassing questions must not be asked when children, for example, are around. This situation whenever it occurs, increases the error margin. In treating sensitive questions, an appropriate environment must be found. This will help the respondent to give meaningful answers. In the field, the fieldworker must operate with care and must estimate the psychology of the people before he introduces his questions.

We must be particularly careful in the application of questionnaire to non-literate people. Very often, the interaction is very unbalanced; at times, the respondents may give spurious answers which they think the fieldworkers want to hear.

In the Ghanaian situation, computer services are now available though expensive. The researcher must be aware that questionnaire data must be processed. Coders must be employed and computer analyst's services must be obtained. If these facilities do not exist, the use of bulky questionnaires is not appropriate. The method and the processes involved in questionnaire construction are time-consuming. This fact must be borne in mind constantly by the researcher.

USE OF DOCUMENTS

All research workers start from the known to the unknown. The researcher does not operate in a vacuum. He must orient himself to the field situation, to research objectives and to methods of social investigation. For these reasons, the field investigator normally consults and reads existing documents. He does not rush into the field without consulting relevant documents.

Scholarship, it is said, is a co-operative enterprise and for that reason, whenever one learns from another author, he must give proper acknowledgement to all the documents and the literature he consulted. Proper footnotes and bibliographical notes must be used in all scientific work of this nature. It is improper to pick ideas from other authors' work without proper acknowledgement.

In going to the field, the researcher consults the literature for past and present studies of relevance. He reads official reports, census data, archival material, statistical data and many related writings. These different sources can help him to outline his ideas in exact and precise forms.

Documents can be used as a source of secondary data. If the problem warrants it and the data exist the use of documentary sources alone may suffice. Such data may be obtained from public institutions, hospitals, records, census and statistical offices. The researcher may also visit relevant institutions to get materials. These materials from well-established institutions are usually reliable because they have been collected with much care and patience. Such data can help him to answer part of his questions. For these reasons, researchers can benefit greatly from the judicious use of institutional secondary data. Historical documents, parliamentary reports, city council deliberations, colonial papers and agreements, statistical reports, minutes of institutions and other related materials can also serve as useful sources of information. The researcher can get additional information from financial institutions, archives, corporations and other private sources. In dealing with human beings, we must be committed to secrecy in confidential matters and we must not reveal the identity of the individual without his express permission.

We can get information from personal letters and other personal documents such as, wills, letters, diaries and personal memoranda. These papers are rich in detail and have built-in reliability. They can give a useful insight into the personal lives of people. They can throw some light on the problem, experiences and rationale underlying some individual's thoughts. These data tend to be free from response bias. They are, therefore, reliable and valid materials. If they can be made available, researchers must take advantage of them to supplement other sources of data collection.

FOCUS GROUP DISCUSSION

Sometimes explanatory research is pursued through the use of focus groups or guided small group discussions. This technique is used frequently in market-oriented research studies. The researcher, may use a focus group that has knowledge about the research topic, to discuss or to seek further information on various aspects of the topic. If, for example, the researcher is introducing a new product for family planning, he needs to find out more about the suitability of the product and an acceptable price and indeed, the suitable way to introduce the commodity. It will be helpful if the researcher gets a focus group of probably knowledgeable sample from the community with whom to discuss the topic in order to gain an intelligible image into the meaning of the topic and its essential components regarding suitability and pricing.

In a focus group, about 6 to 10 people who appear knowledgeable about the topic are brought together to engage them in a guided discussion. Thus, if a researcher will like to find out, in an explanatory way, issues regarding acceptability and pricing of condom, he has to gather together knowledgeable and interested people who wish to control population increase to discuss the topic and to give useful insight and advice. Again, if the topic deals with the selection of chiefs, the researchers must seek knowledge by bringing traditional elders together to discuss the topic. The topics for the group are selected on the basis of relevancy to the aims and objectives of the research.

The participants in a focus group discussion are not chosen on the basis of probability selection; rather it is based on non-probabilistic purposive sampling. For this reason, it is important to select many different focus groups on particular issue under study. Typically, more than one focus group is convened in given research study since one group may not be typical to give the researcher a reliable insight which reflects the community mood to offer any serious generalizable insights.

Built into focus group is cost effective, it is low in cost to get a group to give a serious thought to an issue. It has flexibility and high face validity. It gives an insight into a real life situation in capturing the reality from the group in the actual community. However, the data may be difficult to analyse. For further elucidating see Babbie (1990).

ERRORS IN SOCIAL RESEARCH

There are two main types of errors commonly encountered in social research. They are (1) errors which emanate from ineffective sampling procedures (see the chapter on sampling), and (2) errors coming from non-sampling procedures (see Kish, 1967). These errors are inter-related:

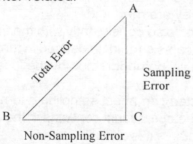

Fig. 4:   Interrelationship of Field Errors.

In Fig. 4, the right-angled triangle is used to indicate the nature of the interrelationship of these field errors through the Pythagoras theorem.

$$AB^2 = BC^2 + AC^2$$

Total Error = Standard Error of Sampling² + Standard Error of Non sampling²

That is to say, to reduce total error, the researcher must concern himself with finding adequate means to improve his sampling technique and his techniques for collecting data. The total error is the sum of the squares of all the discrepancies between the observations and the actual situation the researcher aims to measure. Non-sampling errors can emerge from field techniques, from personal biases, from coding, editing and from the analysis of data.

To reduce total error, therefore, the researcher must improve his sampling and non-sampling techniques. Side AC can be shortened by improvement in sampling procedures, i.e. by taking more sampling units and by using probability sampling techniques. The researcher may reduce non-sampling error Side BC by improving his technique of social investigation and data processing technique. And he must use relevant methods and concepts to collect data.

Measures to Reduce Errors

To reduce error, a meaningful representative sampling must be designed. Kish (1967) mentions three points in this regard:

(1) that the true value of the research must be uniquely defined;
(2) that the true value must be defined in such a manner that the purposes of the survey are met; and
(3) where it is possible to do so consistently with the first two criteria, the research concepts should be defined in terms of operations which can actually be understood by the local.

These measures if neglected can affect sampling and non-sampling frames. For some items, the operational concepts in the situation can be obtained easily but for others it is difficult.

The non-sampling errors emerge from non-coverage, non-response errors in observations, framing of the questionnaire and asking sensitive questions without establishing a field rapport. Errors of non-observation can also result from failure to obtain information from a segment of the survey population.

It is in this sphere that we can distinguish between two sources of non-response error. These are non-coverage and refusals. The former means that there is a failure on the part of the designer to include some units in the actual designing of the sampling frame.

Refusals refer to the failure on the part of the field interviewer to get information from some respondents. It may be due to non-coverage. Incomplete listing is also an outcome of inaccessibility and difficulties in mapping the area. The refusal rate will increase sampling error by decreasing the effectiveness of the calculated sample size and the non-sampling error.

There is also the issue of sampling bias which can arise from inadequate sampling or from faulty sampling design. It may be due to wrong selection procedures and from partial or incomplete enumeration of the selected sampling units. In sampling, therefore, the researcher must include diverse elements in the proportions in which they occur in the actual field situation. Size sample alone is no proof that the estimate will be accurate. Hsin-Pao (1955: 34) opines that "a small sample cross-checked by various methods may produce, under certain circumstances, more accurate and reliable information than a large one". If carefully selected, such a small size is more economical and efficient to handle than a larger one.

Inadequate definitions of operational concepts may also account for errors. Vague concepts may also account for errors. Vague concepts, unclear wording and improper application of theory may tend to distort the focus of the research. Therefore, concepts must always be defined clearly and they must be adequately tested in the field. Where possible local meanings must be applied.

Examples from Field Experiences

Experiences acquired from three social surveys are given below to throw some light on fieldwork and to provide the student of social research with examples of common errors.

1. *Summary on Housing Conditions and Utilization of Health Services*
In 1972, the University of Ghana Medical School, Department of Community Health, asked two research scientists, Drs. E. O. Boateng, Institute of Social, Statistical and Economic Research (I.S.S.E.R.), and P. A. Twumasi, Department of Sociology, to conduct a social survey into "Housing Conditions and Utilization of Health Services with Particular Reference to the Population at Achimota Village, Adabraka and Tesano in Accra". The study was conducted during the long vacation period from June to September 1972.

The scientists were requested to find out the different types of housing conditions in Accra and to show whether there is any difference in health behaviour, with particular reference to utilization of health care facilities by the people who occupy the various types of housing units.

At Achimota Village, we selected a group of people from the Kopevi village sector in Achimota. They were predominantly illiterates. Most of them were self-employed workers in auto-mechanic and carpentry jobs. At Adabraka, the residents were from various ethnic groups. A significant proportion of them were educated and were working in the civil service and other industrial and commercial organizations. At Tesano, the residents were mainly university lecturers, doctors, lawyers and other professionals working in administrative and managerial jobs.

Fifty-two medical students were selected and trained in field techniques including problems of fieldwork, interviewing procedures among others. They were instructed in the psychology of interviewing, how to ask right questions at the appropriate times; they were introduced to measures that could be used to increase field response rate by call back. The students, after training, were put into groups of three. In particular, we took into consideration the nature of the field situation. Those who were familiar with a particular area were selected to work in that area. The language question was also noted. They were conversant with the particular predominant language spoken in the area. They were told to visit households when it is convenient for the head of the household or his representative.

Daily checks were made by the principal investigators. Information collected was checked and edited on daily basis. Incomplete questionnaires were returned and refilled.

We adhered to probability sampling because it is the only approach in sampling methodology that makes possible representative sampling design. The method enables us to check error in an organized systematic way. It enabled us to estimate the extent to which the collected data, based on the estimated sample, were likely to be different from the entire population. In using the probability sampling frame, we expected to get a sample which was not significantly different from the survey population. In order to lower variance within each selected stratum in the survey area, the specific sampling scheme adopted was a stratified one (see Chapter Two). We selected each stratum by the systematic sampling procedure with a random start.

There were differences, however. But these differences between the sampling areas, while allowing us to obtain more information, did not contribute significantly to the sampling error. In fact, it was noted that differences between strata in the population did not contribute to the sampling error of the estimate of the population. Sampling error of the estimate of the population comes in fact from variations among sampling units that are in the same stratum. Hence through stratification, we were able to get homogeneous sampling units.

Where a stratum showed more variability than other strata, a larger sample size was taken; a stratum of less variability got a smaller sample size. This method enabled us to explain variability.

In Achimota Village, we selected 430 respondents; at Adabraka, we selected 1,800 respondents and at Tesano, we selected 370 respondents. However, there was a difference in the response rate. The figures given below show the response and non-response rates (estimated in percentages). The non-response rate was higher in Achimota Village (13.06 per cent) where many of the respondents were found to be illiterates (Table 1).

TABLE 1

Response and Non-Response Rates at Achimota Village, Tesano and Adabraka

Response and Non-response Rates	Achimota Village		Tesano		Adabraka	
	Abs	%	Abs	%	Abs	%
Response	370	86.04	365	98.5	1760	97.5
Non-response	60	13.06	5	1.5	40	2.5
Total	430	100.00	370	100.00	1800	100.00

Source: Calculated from the study by Boateng, E. O. and P. A. Twumasi, 1972. *Community Health Report No. 6,* University of Ghana Medical School, Department of Community Health, Accra.

In both Tesano and Adabraka, the inhabitants were fairly well educated. The response rates were significantly high. What then accounts for the high non-response rate in Achimota Village? Before we attempt to explain the differences in the response rates, it is important to look at similar differences in response rates in two other social surveys.

2.   Traditional Attitudes Towards Health Disease and Family
      Planning
In 1973, the Population Dynamics Programme of the University of
Ghana (in conjunction with the University of North Carolina, Chapel
Hill, U.S.A.) agreed to finance a study into traditional Ghanaian
Communities. The principal investigators were Drs. G. K. Nukunya
and P. A. Twumasi (both of the University of Ghana). We selected
two urban areas and two rural communities.

   (i) *Nsawam* — This is one of the principal towns in the
                  Eastern Region with a population of 25,528
                  (1970).

   (ii) *Dobro* — This is in the Eastern Region. It is situated
                  on the Nsawam-Aburi road. It is a small
                  farming community and the inhabitants
                  were mainly subsistence farmers with a
                  population of 278 inhabitants (1970).

   (iii) *Dzelukofe* — This town has the characteristics of an ur-
                  ban town. It is about 130 kilometres from
                  Accra, with a population of 5,153 people
                  (1970). It is a suburb of Keta, in the Volta
                  Region.

   (iv) *Abor* — This is a rural community in the Volta Re-
                  gion with a population of 3,434 inhabitants
                  (1970). The Ewe inhabitants represent 96.5
                  per cent of the people.

      Table 2 shows clearly the response and non-response rates.
The response rate again was higher in the urban areas than in the
rural areas.

3.   Impact of Tourism on Social Life in Ghana
The third social survey was conducted in June 1974 by a group of
principal investigators headed by Professor N. O. Addo, Director of
Population Dynamics Programme, University of Ghana. The other
principal investigators were Professor George Benneh, Dr. J. M.
Assimeng, Mr. J. Kudadjie, Dr. S. A. Danquah and Dr. P. A. Twumasi.
The purpose of the survey was to study "The Impact of Tourism on

TABLE 2

Response and Non-Response Rates in Four Communities: Nsawam, Dobro, Dzelukofe and Abor

Response and Non-response Rates	Nsawam		Dobro		Dzelukofe		Abor	
	Abs	%	Abs	%	Abs	%	Abs	%
Response	694	99.1	55	78.3	193	96.5	175	92.1
Non-response	6	0.9	15	21.7	7	3.5	15	7.9
Total	700	100.0	70	100.0	200	100.0	190	100.0

Source: Calculated from the study by Dr. Nukunya, G. K. and Dr. P. A. Twumasi, 1974. *Traditional Attitudes Towards Health Disease and Family Planning in Four Selected Ghanaian Communities,* Legon Population Dynamics Programme Study.

Social Life in Ghana". The research was commissioned by the Ghana Tourist Control Board.

The sample areas included both urban centres and rural communities. All the regional capitals were included in the sample. Some villages in the regions were also included. Villages were selected, one from each region, to act as control to determine if there was a difference between rural and urban views towards tourism and the tourist trade.

The field assistants were recruited from the University of Ghana. They were given an intensive orientation course in field psychology and research techniques. They were distributed, at the end of their training, to the selected areas for interviewing and assisting respondents to fill questionnaire schedules.

During the fieldwork, many of the field assistants complained about difficulties in contacting rural and urban respondents. Recalls were made, substitute samples were framed and interviewers re-entered the field where necessary. They were closely supervised. Eventually, there was some improvement in the urban response rate; but in the rural areas, the difficulties in reaching some of the rural respondents remained. Part of the reason was that many of the rural respondents were not found at home during interviews. This fact was borne out by data from Paga in the Upper Region, Ewhia in the Ashanti Region and Kato in the Brong-Ahafo Region. These communities are rural, inhabited mainly by farmers. Our attention was drawn to the fact that there is a need to be more careful in studying rural people, especially illiterates who have a different style of life.

Data cited in the last few pages clearly throw some light on the differences in response rates in rural and urban areas. Future research workers should take into consideration the nature of these observed differences in order to improve the quality and the quantity of collected information.

A possible explanation of the difference is partly ecological. In the urban situation, we have large dense permanent settlements. The buildings are relatively well outlined. The area maps are specific. The houses are numbered. In the rural areas, some of the houses are not numbered. The buildings are often scattered. The people are mainly subsistence farmers and they have different work culture and habits. They go to their farms during the best part of the day, returning late in the evening. Some may even choose to stay with other farming relatives especially during planting and harvesting seasons. Besides, rural folks have been noticed to shy away from answering embarrassing questions. Wrong identity of the interviewer and wrong wording may also play a part in refusals. One of the field interviewers had this to say: "Some of us were mistaken for tax collectors, so they refused to answer our questions".

In small scale social surveys (unlike census studies, in which the mass media and other government publicity media assist to persuade the local inhabitants to remain in their homes), we tend to get poor publicity. As a factor, lack of publicity increases the non-response rate.

The travelling arrangements, work habits and personal sensitivities about answering certain research questions account for higher non-response rates. In the urban areas, the respondents tend to share a similar orientation as the field interviewer. He understands the interviewer and tend to co-operate because he knows the meaning of the research studies. Questions about sex and other related sensitive matters are freely discussed.

We may say then that different culture, norms and values account for the discrepancies between the response rates in the two cultural settings. In carrying out field research, therefore, the field scientist must of necessity use culturally-relevant field methods in the collection of field material.

SUMMARY OF FIELD STRATEGY

The initial problem is to select an appropriate research topic. The selection of the research topic needs some thought. For example, are the people likely to have answers to the research problem? What methods can be used to extract the field material? The ability to perceive a relevant problem whose solution has a bearing on the situation is a good starting point in any field research.

After the selection process, there is the need to specify and define crucial research concepts and variables. The concepts must be defined empirically and translated into the appropriate local languages. Testable indicators must be defined. The prevailing social mood must be assessed. The empirical definition must be relevant to the prevailing social mood. One way to achieve this is to carry out a pre-test. The social indicators or the operational concepts must be tested in the local situation.

The methods for data collection must also receive considerable attention. In rural society, the majority of the people cannot read and write, therefore, we must use more of the interviewing method than the formal questionnaire method.

The common techniques used in rural research are field interviewing, the use of questionnaires, participant observation, and focus group discussions. It is important to use more than one method in collecting field data.

Chapter 4

MODALITIES FOR ENTERING RURAL COMMUNITIES

INTRODUCTION

Researchers must know the characteristics and behaviour patterns of rural people. In my own experience, a number of rural research projects have failed or have met with many pragmatic difficulties because researchers, who are often urban based, do not appreciate rural usages and nuances. This chapter is meant to give an insight into common characteristics of rural people and their settlements.

CHARACTERISTICS OF RURAL AREAS

In 1984, the census figures had indicated that about 70 per cent of Ghanaians live in rural and outlying areas. A rural area was defined as any settlement which had a population of less than 5,000 inhabitants. Indeed about 50 per cent of rural settlements had a population of less than 2,000 inhabitants. From a sociological view point, the smallness of the population in each settlement exhibits the following characteristics.

Kinship

The interactive mode of behaviour is face to face. The people live together in kinship based communal houses. Nearly every house has a large compound where relatives from both patrilineal and matrilineal households interact on a daily basis. In the large compound, a researcher is able to determine the actual composition of each household, the head of the household and indeed, at the larger level of relationship, the head of the family (the lineage) will also be known.

One lineage is one blood, as the saying goes, is interpreted to mean that in decision-making what the head of the family says in the final analysis carries weight. Individual input into the decision-making process is recognized but when a decision on important issues are taken it carries weight because it is supported by the elders.

Homogeneity of Population

Another important characteristic is the homogeneity of the population. The majority of the people in a rural settlement comes from one principal ethnic group. If a fieldworker goes to another part of Ghana to undertake a fieldwork, he or she would find that the majority of the inhabitants or almost all speak the same local language and that they exhibit similar cultural characteristics. Ghana is divided into regions, districts and constituencies. The ten regions are: Greater Accra, Volta, Western, Eastern, Central Ashanti, Brong Ahafo, Northern, Upper East and Upper West. They are further sub-divided into 110 districts. Out of the districts are the constituencies, which are largely homogenous in terms of ethnicity. Thus, for the fieldworker, an insight into the principal local languages is an advantage. It is from this point of view that research scientists and field assistants so employed for research work must speak the local language in that locality.

Structure of Housing

Another problem area is the numbering of the houses or even how to define a house and a household. In a typical village, the boundaries of houses are not clearly defined. One house may lead into another compound. Relatives from other houses may move up and down from their living quarters to other houses to perform some of their day to day activities. For these reasons, a fieldworker must undertake a feasibility study to become aware of these social facts in order to help him to obtain a real insight into the definition of a house, composition of a household, types of lineage groups and consequently get acquainted with the social composition and interactive daily arrangements of rural inhabitants.

RURAL NUANCES

Level of Development

In a fieldwork situation, apart from understanding the social networking, there is the need for an understanding of the sensitivities of the people as well as the psychological make up. Rural people, like all peoples, are suspicious of strangers, the degree of suspicion is greater among rural inhabitants than among urban dwellers.

Introducing Oneself

When a fieldworker enters a village or a small town, people begin to wonder about the mission of the fieldworker. The gossips start and interpretation and reinterpretation of the situation begin. It is precisely because of this situation which may give birth to misformation that necessitates the fieldworker to enter the village properly.

When a person enters the field, he must give a proper account of himself. He must introduce himself to the proper power structure in the community, i.e. the legitimate chief, his elders, village committee leaders or other prominent leaders of the community, in order to gain a legitimate entry into the community. The objective of the project must be known together with its applied implications. If the objective of the project is known, then unnecessary suspicion will be discarded. This introductory formality will give the field researcher the passport to enter into the chosen community.

It is always good to go to the village with a reliable contact person preferably from the village or at least the district. Such a person would be able to inform the fieldworker on the right procedure to follow, the type of people to meet and how to strategize for the fieldwork and the interviews. It must also be mentioned that contact persons must be selected with great care and understanding of the village's social structure. The principle is that it is through the contact persons that reliable information and respondents would be reached for the interview. In a rural social situation, the role of the legitimate chief, his elders and heads of household is an important factor. They are of great assistance in helping the researcher to obtain the needed information. They are also important conduit through which a researcher can establish the needed rapport. All these factors in entering the field must be understood by the researcher if he does a feasibility study and has met the right contact persons to brief him or her in understanding the particular field situation.

Settling to Work

Then, the field worker must settle down to do some serious fieldwork. His life style and general approach to field work must fit what the local people expect. He must find a place to live. Usually the chief is a good contact man. Kinship plays an important part in local activities. The researcher must be careful not to offend any person. He must be fair and objective in his relationship with the people. If he has the use of a motor vehicle, for example, he may be asked to give "lifts" to people in the village who may urgently need such assistance. If he does a favour to one section of the community, he must be prepared to do likewise to other community members in similar situations in order to maintain good field relations.

It is also good in the collection of reliable and valid data to know about the daily habits and whereabouts of the local inhabitants, their time preferences and the right time to meet them to carry out the interviews.

Timing of Research Project

The timing of a research study is of great importance in the collection of reliable and valid information. The general principle is that the researcher must enter the field to meet with the respondents at a convenient time to them. For example, in a rural community most of the people classified as respondents tend to be farmers and fishermen and women. Most of the day they are usually at their work places away from their usual residential places. The whereabouts of the people must be known. It is usually important to survey the field in order to determine a convenient time to reach the people in a village community.

It is difficult to collect field data during the raining season. During the raining season, the ground is soak and wet, household daily routine is often disturbed. Some members of a household may move to stay with other relatives. All these issues which will disturb normal social interaction must be taken into account in determining an appropriate period and time to enter into the field.

This discussion throws some light on the position of the researcher who goes to the field in a rural setting. It represents a commitment to actively collect consistent and valid material. It means precisely that the researcher must intimately be acquainted with the aspirations of the people, must understand the language of the people, the meaning they give to social situation and must learn to view the social world of the respondents from the way they structure their own experiences. It means that the researcher must be humble enough to learn from the field. This is so because from a different social background, one must be extremely careful not to impose his own value orientation on the social situation. The point to be remembered in this regard is that the observer is in a relatively different social position when he goes to the rural field. He must not look down on the people he is studying. He must, in all humility, learn to accept and to collect data in a well-thought out way. This is the true vocation of the social scientist.

Chapter 5

ANALYSIS OF DATA

INTRODUCTION

When the scientist returns from the field he must settle down to analyze the data. The process (of data analysis) is a continuous one involving many stages. At every stage, the researcher must ask questions relating to his objectives in order to obtain meaningful answers. In this regard, the principal concepts in the study's objectives must be used to examine the data.

The stages are editing, tabulation, coding and computer processing. The last stages are resorted to if questionnaires were used in seeking field information. The process of data analysis requires skills, patience and thoroughness.

EDITING

The data must be examined for consistency of responses. The researcher must read through all the data in order to determine whether the replies are worthwhile. He examines the data to find out whether all the questions have been answered properly. They are carefully checked to determine how far they are accurate, consistent and appropriate. In certain cases, the editor may be able to provide intelligent answers to blank columns after following the trend of thought of the interviewee. He must, however, be extremely careful in his editing work. If there is any doubt, he must ask his assistants to go back to the field to check. In areas where the researcher is not the editor, he takes appropriate measures to train intelligent assistants to play such a role. It is the work of the editing staff to examine all the answers obtained from the field in order to set the stage for coding. The staff goes through the original questions to determine the relevancy of the answers. Then the main trends of the answers (for open-ended and pre-coded types of questions (see chapter 3, the section which deals with the questionnaire method) are recorded.

In small scale field surveys, especially in areas where the

questionnaire method was not used to gather information, the researcher does not have to go through the processes of coding, and computer processing. In this regard, from the editing stage, he starts to classify and tabulate the main information.

TABULATION

Tabulation is the process whereby the researcher summarizes quantitative data into statistical tables. For example, in a village survey, information may be obtained on sex, education, occupation and on religious affiliation of the inhabitants. In this context, it possible to summarize the characteristics of the inhabitants into statistical tables. The following tables illustrate tabulation. Table 3 shows there are more females than males in the village. In absolute terms there are hundred more females than males. Overall, 55.5 per cent of the inhabitants are female while 44.5 per cent are male.

TABLE 3

Sex Differential in Village A

Sex	Frequencies	
	Number	%
Male	400	44.5
Female	500	55.5
Total	900	100.0

Table 4 shows that the majority of the inhabitants in the village were illiterates (88.9 per cent); only a few of them had formal education (11.1 per cent).

The third set of characteristics (occupation) can be described in a similar way. Table 5 shows the occupational characteristics of the inhabitants.

It indicates that the majority of the inhabitants (94.4 per cent) are engaged in farming. As a typical village, this finding is not surprising because in Ghana, many of the inhabitants are farm workers. Only 5.6 per cent of the people are engaged in non-farming activities. They are teachers and other clerical workers.

TABLE 4

Educational Characteristics of Village A

Education	Frequencies	
	Number	%
Illiterates	800	88.9
Literates	100	11.1
Total	900	100.0

TABLE 5

Occupational Characteristics of the Inhabitants in Village A

Occupation	Frequencies	
	Number	%
Farmers	850	94.4
Clerical workers	35	3.8
Teachers	15	1.8
Total	900	100.0

The last characteristic is the religious affiliation of the inhabitants.

Table 6 shows the religious characteristics of the people in the village. Of all the religious groups, the catholics are in the majority while the apostolics and the traditionalists are few.

Simple statistical tables can be used to describe the social background of a people. However, it must be remembered that not all the factors in a given survey can be subjected to a statistical treatment. For example, the values and beliefs of a people can best be described and explained in qualitative terms.

The advantage of the statistical method lies in its precision and clarity. It presents numerical evidence in a convincing way. As said earlier, there are difficulties and even misrepresentation if the researcher resorts to express and interpret all social phenomena by numbers and tables. Many social conditions and variations of life cannot be fully and accurately expressed in arithmetical terms. Therefore, statistical calculations have limited use and must be used with care and understanding (Hsin-Pao 1955: 71).

TABLE 6

Religious Characteristics of the Inhabitants in Village A

Religion	Frequencies	
	Number	*%*
Catholics	400	44.4
Presbyterians	300	33.3
Methodists	100	11.3
Traditionalists	50	5.5
Apostolics	50	5.5
Total	900	100.0

CODING PROCEDURE

Coding is a system for preparing quantitative analysis of data. It uses numbers to symbolize words. In the exercise of translating words into numbers, a scheme called coding instruction is prepared to direct the process. The coded material is then fed into the computer direct from the questionnaire or interview schedule. Coding requires expert knowledge and skill and may be omitted in many social surveys. If the researcher wishes to use the coding method he must consult an expert. Returning to the process, the coder assigns a number or a symbol to each category of the questionnaire answers.

The first step in coding procedure is to provide a coding frame, or what is sometimes called the coding scheme. The scheme is used as a guide to help the coder to translate the responses (in the questionnaire) into numbers. Each question and its answer must be carefully examined. For example, if one asks the question: what is your age? he must look for all the possible answers given by the respondent. If he gets an age range of 15 to 60, he need to group these data before he assigns coding symbols to them: The ages may be grouped in the following ways:

15–19
20–24

25–29
30–34
35–39
40–44
45–49
50–54
55–59
60–64

Each cluster of age group is given a code number. To 15–19, we assign 01 to the next group we assign 02 etc. (because the variables are more than 9).

After going through all the questions, in a similar manner, the symbols are put into a standard coding scheme (Table 7). At this point, trained coding assistants are employed to work on it.

In pre-coded question, where there are only few answers, the preparation of a coding scheme raises no major difficulties. From the field answers, the coders assign numbers to each of the questions; then they are translated to the standard coding format. But in the open-ended questions, the answers are of a varied nature; therefore, they require a thorough check in order to determine the main trends before one embarks on the preparation of a coding scheme.

Many of the difficulties which may occur in coding arise from inadequate preparation of the field questionnaire. They may be unrelated to the objectives of the study. Therefore, if questions are to be coded, great care must be taken to construct them.

Let us give an example of a coding scheme and its preparation. The following questions can guide us in the preparation of coding scheme. (1) Sex; (2) age; (3) ethnic affiliation; (4) citizenship; (5) occupation; (6) marital status; (7) number of wives; (8) children; (9) clan membership; (10) religion; (11) medical attention sought when ill; (12) social activities; (13) educational standing; and (14) social problems in the town. After examining the answers given by the respondents, the researcher prepares the following coding scheme.

After the preparation of the coding scheme, trained coders or coding assistants are instructed to use the coding frame, as a guide, to code all the survey's questionnaire on the standard coding sheets. They need constant supervision. Through the use of computer

TABLE 7

A Coding Scheme

Question	Col.	Code Description
Serial No. Household 3 cols. individual 2 cols.	1–5	Identification
Question 1. Sex	6	1. Male 2. Female
Question 2. Age	7–8	Code actual years
Question 3. Ethnicity	9	1. Ashanti 2. Other (specify)
Question 4. Citizenship	10	1. Juaso 2. non-Juaso (specify)
Question 5. Occupation	11	0. Labourer 1. Farmer 2. Trader 3. Clerk 4. Teacher 5. Other (specify)
Question 6. Marital status	12	1. Married 2. Single 3. Divorced 4. Widowed 5. Separated
Question 7. Number of wives	13	0. Not applicable 1. Single 2. Plural
Question 8. No. of Children	14–15	Code actual number
Question 9. Clan membership	16	0. Unknown 1. Oyoko 2. Ekoona 3. Asona 4. Asene 5. Agona 6. Bretuo 7. Tena 8. Aduana 9. Other (specify)

TABLE 7(Cont'd.)

Questions 10. Religion	17	1. Catholic 2. Presbyterian 3. Moslem 4. Traditional 5. Other (specify)
Question 11. Medical attention	18	1. Traditional 2. Scientific 3. Both (Traditional and Scientific)
Question 12. Social activities	19	0. Not applicable 1. Church 2. Drumming 3. Funeral 4. Organist — Concert 5. Clubs 6. Games and Sports 7. Dancing 8. Cinema, Parties 9. Drinking
Question 13. Education	20	1. Illiterate 2. Literate
Question 14. If literate specify	21	0. Not applicable 1. Up to JSS 3 2. Up to SSS 3 3. Up to Polytechnic 4. Up to University 5. Other (specify)
Question 15. Specification of crucial problem in Juaso	22	0. Disunity among people 1. Chieftaincy 2. Litigation 3. Lack of electricity 4. Lack of social amenities 5. Sanitation 6. Truancy on the part of youth 7. Lack of water — pipe borne 8. Lack of high institution of education 9. Hospital facilities — high cost of living.

softwares e.g. SPSS, coding of responses on standard coding sheets can be by-passed.

ANALYSIS

Analysis means a critical examination of material in order to understand its parts and its relationship and to discover its trends. It means the separation of the research data into its constituent parts. After the separation, the researcher must study the nature of the material to determine its essential features and their relations.

Types of Analysis

There are two types of analysis: qualitative and quantitative analyses.

Qualitative Analysis

In qualitative analysis, the researcher, after the collection of qualitative data, must examine the main features of the material. For example, in a field survey to study the attitudes of a group of people towards family planning, the researcher must examine all the responses or the answers he has collected from the field. In order to proceed in an orderly fashion, he must look at the study's objective (see Chapter 1). Let us assume that it is one of his objectives to describe the social background of the people. In this case he must examine the variables dealing with the social characteristics.

In sociological analysis, one needs to know the background of the people to examine their response towards family planning. If some of the people are christians, then we need to determine whether there is any difference between Christian and non-Christian views towards family planning. After this discovery, if any, the researcher needs to offer a sociological explanation to throw light on the difference between Christian and non-Christian views. Sociological explanation is necessary because the final aim of social research is to derive a sociological generalization from the observed facts. In other words, from an analysis of the qualitative information, the scientist must generalize his findings based on the facts. In attempting to generalize, one must be extremely careful.

The data must be sufficient, the sample area must be seen to be adequately representative of the group and the answers must be checked in terms of their appropriateness. Also, the researcher must compare his findings with other existing theories or information.

Quantitative Data

The other analysis deals with quantitative material. Usually, this material is processed by the computer. A typical example of this type of material is obtained through the use of questionnaires. As said before, after coding and computer analysis of the material, the researcher obtains the statistical marginals. These marginals are already analyzed in terms of percentages and absolute numbers. The work of the researcher is simplified. His main concern, at this stage, is to derive the trends of the analysis and to offer explanations and generalizations based on it.

The essential variables in the researcher's objectives are important ideas employed to examine the material. The researcher finds out from the assembled material what is typical and why others deviate from the norm. Then he attempts to explain variations. He is interested in averages and variations. He is interested in social phenomena and examines how the phenomena affect patterns of social relationships. This examination will enable him to understand the phenomena and to explain and attempt to make predictions. Analysis, therefore, helps the researcher to eliminate unlikely possibilities so that he may guard against spurious relationships.

Cross Tabulation Analysis

The important issue in field research is the ability to establish a relationship between dependent and independent variables. It is the starting point in affirming a hypothesis or negating the hypothesis so derived from a theory. In order to establish a relationship, the researcher must indicate in the tool of measurement (for example in the questionnaire) the background characteristics of the respondents. For example, as a result of the age differential or religious background and/or education voting pattern to district assembly or to parliament will be understood. Such background characteristics will be matched and analyzed against the real voting behaviour. This type of analysis is termed cross-tabulation analysis.

a.

Age	Voting Pattern
Young	87%
Old	14%

b.

Religion	Voting Pattern
Christian	46%
Moslem	54%

In establishing relationships, there is the need to look closely at possible factors, by stratifying. Relationships are established by use of cross-tabulations of two or more variables. For example, one may find an apparent relationship between two variables i.e. "the young and the love for pop music". He may stratify the component variable "young" into "literate young" and "illiterate young". Then he may wish to determine whether the love for pop music exists at the two levels. If it exists, it strengthens the relationship so that a firm generalization can be established.

Hypothesis Testing

Hypothesis is usually derived from a theory. It states a tentative relationship between two variables: dependent and an independent variable. For example, in Fig. 3, the discussion threw some light on the need to derive a hypothesis from a theory in a logical fashion. The relationship between the dependent and independent variables must be tested from the empirical data through statistical method. In a study by Twumasi and Nukunya (1975), one of the stated hypothesis was that in psychological diseases, people will tend to frequent traditional healers. Statistical evidence must be obtained from the field and tested statistically.

Analysis is not done in an *ad hoc* fashion. All researchers must carefully think about the analytical categories used in classifying data; because they affect assumptions underlying analytical procedures.

THE USE OF COMPUTER

The computer is a friend of the researcher and it is, therefore, imperative in this day and age that the social researcher must become conversant with its use. It is for this reason that all research students at under-graduate and graduate levels must be introduced to the computer.

At the outset of a research project, the categories must be clearly stated to enable the computer programmer to arrange the material to be fed into the computer to produce the needed data from the marginal as well as from the cross tabulation analysis. That is to say, the initial stage of the fieldwork the researcher must decide on the use of the computer to help in the analysis of the data. Some research scientists are even predisposed to the use of the computer that they may wish to carry the computer to the field to key in the field answers. It makes it easier in the compilation of the data and subsequently, in the data analysis. The analytical material is also safely stored in the computer machine. This aspect of the security of the data-information is so crucial to the researcher. It helps the researcher enormously in safeguarding his research data. A word of caution is also necessary to protect the material so saved in the computer so that what is safely stored is not erased away due to negligence, shortage of electric power and forgetfulness.

In the write up of the research report, computer usage has become very important. The typing must be set in the computer to make it easier for corrections to be made. It is for these reasons that it is necessary for all research scientists to take a course (or courses) in the usage of computers. The statistical figures compiled by the computers tend to be almost always reliable, though it must be emphasized that what you feed into the computer is indeed what you get out.

Research students will need appropriate training in the application of computer programmes and packages. It is useful also for students to be aware of the existence and use of various computer packages.

The pace of computer development and dissemination of knowledge in today's world is fast. It is, therefore, difficult to anticipate the kind of equipment that may be available to a social researcher and with which he/she will be able to work. As a result of this tendency, it is useful to provide an overview of the stages in the evolution of computers in social research work.

Though the history of computers started in the 19th century, most data analyses conducted with the help of computers is a recent phenomenon. Computer programming goes through data manipulation, beyond simple counting and sorting to the performance of intricate computation and the presentation of sophisticated results. A computer can be programmed to look into several variables simultaneously and to compute a variety of statistical information and relationships. Computers can calculate complex statistics, a good deal faster and more accurately than former human methods. There are indeed a number of computer programmes available these days that it is advisable for the social researcher to be familiar with and to utilize in analysis of data.

It is necessary for the social scientist to be familiar with the use of one of the most popular computer softwares such as the Statistical Package for the Social Scientist (SPSS). The researcher must get the sense of how SPSS works. This insight will help the researcher to understand the general logic in the use of the computer in carrying out data analysis, before, during and after field work (Babbie, 1995).

The purpose of any serious research investigation includes the design and implementation of the data procedures, the management of the data so collected and indeed an analysis of the accumulated data. It is also part of the research work to explore, to describe and to offer explanation for the analytical pattern so observed. It is therefore necessary to analyze the data critically and sufficiently as per the research objectives. With the use of the SPSS the researcher will be able to accomplish these aims and objectives of the research in an efficient and effective manner. All one needs to know is to master the programme SPSS commands, and learn a little on how to create and manage the files at the computer end. The researcher must have a clear understanding of what to get out of the research investigation. The computer and the SPSS package are simply the tools that can help the researcher to summarize the data, to create the appropriate tables, the graphs, to examine the relationships among the variables, to perform other tests of statistical significance based on the field hypotheses and to develop and create models. The researcher is, therefore, advised to learn the SPSS software, which includes a lot of commands and procedures.

Chapter 6

THE WRITING OF RESEARCH REPORT

INTRODUCTION

In writing a research report, the author must state the problem(s) to which the study is directed, the research questions with which he is dealing (whether or not he has specific hypotheses that are being tested) and the relevant theoretical concepts which are being used to guide the work. He states the sampling criteria and sampling procedure (why and how he selected the respondents). He collates the various sources of data and analyzes the data and states the significance of his findings, especially in relation to the issues, problems and concepts that are in his objectives. He must answer certain questions. How valid and reliable are the findings? Can the findings be generalized beyond the particular research setting? Do they suggest other studies to be conducted?

A *brief* synopsis of the study (not more than 3–4 paragraphs) must also be provided. The sources of information that have shaped the study should be listed in alphabetical order and should have been referred to in the body of the report in the appropriate place.

An appendix should be provided for any detailed information which would otherwise distract the reader if put in the body of the report. For example, if one uses a questionnaire or interview schedule, a copy of this form would usually be placed in an appendix.

THE REPORT

After the analysis is completed, the researcher begins to write the formal report. He needs to assemble his data, the statistical tables, if any, and any other evidence. He must remember at this point to relate his findings to other existing body of knowledge. The art of writing is not easy. It needs skill, style and knowledge of the subject matter. In serious writing of this nature, the author must be extremely careful to follow a systematic format. He must proceed with care and with logic. He must use a simple but clear style of writing. He must read over his work several times to make the necessary editorial and structural corrections.

Format of the Research Report

Firstly, the researcher states in an introductory form what the report is about. He states clearly his research problem and his research objectives. Secondly, he indicates what has been done in the area of his research. This means that the review of existing literature must be thoroughly done to throw light on the current study. Thirdly, the researcher must outline his conceptual model, that is, the variables he intends to use and must define the variables clearly to avoid confusion. Fourthly, he must state the specific methods he uses to collect and to analyze the data.

The above outline shows the essential components of a research report. It gives the reader some insight into the methods and techniques used to collect and analyze data and to come to conclusions. The essence of research, it must be emphasized, is to follow systematic and well organized methods of enquiry.

ILLUSTRATIVE ARTICLES OF ACTUAL RESEARCH REPORT

In order to gain an insight into research report writing, three illustrative reports are presented. The first two reports by P. A. Twumasi and J. S. Sinclair are complete research reports while the third article is a chapter in an MSc (Sociology) thesis by K. M. Ganu. Readers should read these articles carefully noting the various points outlined above. It must be noted that for the purpose of this book, the articles have been slightly edited.

1.   *Some Social Characteristic of Ghanaian Medical Students: Towards an Understanding of Medical Socialization*

P. A. Twumasi*

Introduction

The principal concern of this paper is to discuss some of the social characteristics of Ghanaian medical students and to throw some light on the socialization process in medical education. For an understanding of medical

* Then, Senior Lecturer, Department of Sociology, University of Ghana, Legon. This article was first published in *Universitas*, Vol. 5 No.2 1976.

socialization, it is necessary to present supporting facts and figures to give an insight into the social background of Ghanaian medical students.

The period under consideration is from 1964 to 1974. It must be remembered in this regard that the first medical school enrolment started in 1964. It was in October of that year that 35 students were accepted to undertake a two-year pre-clinical course in the University of Ghana. Since then, there has been a continuous inflow of medical students registered in the University of Ghana Medical School with an average intake of 50 students per academic year. According to the University of Ghana Medical School Handbook (issued by the office of the Dean, p.3), the school is well established and there are 14 departments and over 80 per cent of the faculty are Ghanaians.

The method used in the collection of data was mainly of the ex-post facto type. By the kind permission of Professor S. R. A. Dodu, Dean of the School, I was allowed to study the existing records and files to compile the necessary facts and figures. The records were in good order. This helped us to compile the statistical tables within the period of two months of fieldwork. The author was able to listen to and discuss pertinent views expressed by both medical students and faculty on some aspects of medical socialization. These processes of data collection helped us to achieve a significant degree of reliability in the collected field data.

Medical Socialization

Many authors who have worked in the field of medical socialization have argued quite convincingly, with the supporting facts and figures, that there is an interesting relationship between social class and medical admission. In a survey of physicians undertaken in 1962 by the Royal Commission on Health Services in Canada, each student who was admitted into Medicine was asked to fill a questionnaire to show his father's or guardian's occupation at the time the respondent entered a medical school. The data on occupational stratification were arranged into seven occupational classes according to the weight given to each occupation's socio-economic index. This was based on such indicators as education, income and prestige of occupation.[1] It was discovered that medical students were mainly recruited from the upper social strata of society (Table 8).

This type of relationship was also evident when Robert Merton examined the admission procedure of students in the United States. The occupational background of the fathers of the medical students was analyzed and the recognized relationship confirmed the existing notion.[2] Ellis[3] in his "Tomorrow's Doctors" mentioned that this positive relationship existed in Britain. The finding was that medical students tended to be recruited from the upper classes in their society.

The data cited above indicate that medical students tend to be re-

TABLE 8*

Percentage Distribution of General Practitioners and Specialists for Canada by Occupational Group of Father at Entering University, 1962

Occupational Group	Practitioners	Specialists
1. Managerial/Pro	54.4	65.8
2. Clerical/Sales	12.4	11.9
3. Transport/Services	3.7	2.7
4. Craftsmen	9.9	8.4
5. Farmers/Workers	16.4	8.7
6. Fishermen	0.9	0.9
7. Labourers	2.3	1.3
Total	100.0	99.7

Source: Blishen, B. R., 1969. *Doctors and Doctrine.* Toronto: University of Toronto Press, p.33.

cruited mainly from higher socio-economic groups in Euro-American societies. More than half of those who graduated in 1960 from Canadian and
American universities had parents who were professionally trained. As opined
by Oswald Hall,[4] the process of recruitment into medicine, the choice by
persons of a medical career and progressive commitment to the medical
profession appeared to gain particular consideration. Many of them tend to
come from families where the father or a close relative is a practicing physician. Oswald Hall goes on to say:

> . . . one can see why doctors tend to be recruited from the families of professional
> workers. The latter possess the mechanism for generating and nurturing the medical
> ambition. Only members of the profession can translate the public protestations of
> the profession into the vernacular or useful advice. In most cases, family or friends
> played a significant role by envisaging the career line and reinforcing the efforts of
> the recruit. They accomplished the latter by giving encouragement, helping establish
> the appropriate routines, arranging the necessary privacy, discouraging anoma-
> lous behaviour and refining the day to day rewards.[5]

Other students have no such advantages; they tend to make their decisions
to enter medicine somewhat later.[6]

The Ghanaian Situation

Much of the research done by sociologists on medical socialization has

* Tables 8–13 refer to Tables 1–6 in the original.

concerned itself with Euro-American tradition. We need to find out if, and how far, similar conclusions are verifiable in our environment. Given the fact that in our society higher education is free, it is the hypothesis of this paper that the suggestion that students will tend to come from the higher socio-economic class is not tenable at present. As a result of the free education scheme during the First Republic, students in the universities are recruited from all parts of the social and economic system in the Ghanaian society. What we find important is to test the hypothesis that (1) There is a positive relationship between students' performance at sixth form schools and admission into Medical Schools. (2) That certain schools in Ghana, because they have good facilities for teaching science subjects, tend to prepare many more students for medical education. (3) That the sex differential is not an important factor in medical education. There is no remarkable difference between male and female entry performance. (4) That social class background is not an important consideration in Ghanaian medical recruitment, though in future the social class factor will play an important part because secondary education is becoming expensive.

Data were compiled on the following characteristics of the medical students (1) year of admission (2) age differential (3) school attended (4) grades obtained at G.C.E. 'A' Levels (5) male and female distribution of students and (6) occupational background of parents of students. In all, 501 students were covered during the period. As indicated in Table 9, the age distribution of students in the Ghana Medical School at the time they were admitted 1964–1974 shows that a majority of the students were in the 21–25 age group. Out of the total coverage of 501 students, 374 (74.4 per cent) were in the age group of 21–25 years; 122 (24.4 per cent) were in the age group of 16–20 years and 5 (0.9 per cent) of them were found to be above 26 years of age. These age differentials are identical with Jahoda,[7] Peil[8] and Amoa's findings,[9] insofar as the bulk of the students were recruited from the 21–25 age group. What is new is that a significant proportion is also from the 16–20 age group.

Students obtained their secondary and sixth form education from such schools as Mfantsipim, Adisadel, Prempeh College, Accra Academy, Mawuli, Aburi Girls, Wesley Girls, Ghana National, Opoku Ware, St. Augustine's, Achimota, Bishop Herman, Tamale Secondary School and St. John's Secondary School. A few had their education from foreign schools. Of all the local schools, Prempeh College, Achimota, Mfantsipim and Adisadel were in the lead (in this order of priority listing: see Table 10 for the detailed analysis).

Students have offered three or four of the following subjects for admission into the Medical School: Chemistry, Biology, Physics, Maths, Botany and Zoology. Of the total number of responses (1288). 8.8 per cent had grade A at the G.C.E. Advanced Level Examination, 31.4 per

TABLE 9

Age Distribution of Medical Students

AGE		1964	1965	1966	1967	1968	1969	1970	1971	1972	1973	1974	TOTAL
16–20	No.	2	4	5	15	13	14	13	13	8	18	17	122
	%	1.6	3.3	4.1	12.3	10.7	11.5	10.7	10.7	6.4	14.8	13.9	100.0
21–25	No.	35	26	22	37	30	44	38	29	47	31	35	374
	%	9.3	6.9	5.9	9.8	8.1	11.8	10.2	7.8	12.6	8.3	9.3	100.0
26–30	No.	1	—	—	—	2	—	2	—	—	—	—	5
	%	20.0	—	—	—	40.0	—	40.0	—	—	—	—	100.0
31–	No.	—	—	—	—	—	—	—	—	—	—	—	—
	%	—	—	—	—	—	—	—	—	—	—	—	—
Total	No.	38	30	27	52	45	58	53	42	55	49	52	501
	%	7.4	5.9	5.4	10.4	8.9	11.8	10.6	8.4	11	9.8	10.4	100.0

1. Male mean age   —   24
2. Female mean age —   20

TABLE 10

Principal Schools in Ghana and their Quota to the Ghana Medical School 1964–74

Year	Mfa	Adi	Pre	Aca	Maw	Abu	Wes	Nat	Opo	St. A	Ach	Her	Tam	St. J	Oth	Total
1964	6	5	7	—	1	—	1	—	5	2	7	—	1	—	3	38
1965	3	3	7	—	1	2	1	1	1	—	7	—	1	—	3	30
1966	3	1	5	—	—	1	2	—	—	—	6	—	1	1	7	27
1967	10	9	9	2	2	—	1	—	1	1	3	—	1	—	13	52
1968	8	5	6	1	2	—	—	3	4	2	9	2	2	—	4	45
1969	5	2	9	1	5	1	4	2	2	2	5	1	2	—	16	58
1970	5	4	3	1	2	1	4	2	1	2	5	1	1	3	18	53
1971	3	—	2	1	2	—	2	2	—	1	4	1	—	—	23	42
1972	8	5	4	2	1	5	1	11	6	5	7	2	—	2	6	55
1973	8	4	4	1	1	1	1	1	1	—	10	4	1	1	11	49
1974	7	2	9	1	5	—	2	1	1	3	2	2	1	3	13	52
Total	63	40	65	10	22	12	19	11	22	18	64	13	11	10	121	501

Mfa = Mfantsipim
Adi = Adisadel
Pre = Prempeh
Aca = Accra Academy

Abu = Aburi Girls
Wes = Wesley Girls
Nat = Ghana National
Opo = Opoku Ware

Ach = Achimota
Her = Bishop Herman
Tam = Tamale Secondary
St. J = St. John

cent got 'B' Grades, 23.9 per cent had 'C' grades, 23.3 per cent had 'D' grades and 12.5 per cent had 'E' grades. In other words, 64.1 per cent of them had A, B and C grades in their selected subjects for the study of medicine (see Table 11). This is not surprising because it is a known fact that medical students are usually science students with high 'A' level grades. The science students who get admitted into the University of Ghana Medical School have attained a higher academic excellence than their counterparts who were admitted to read B.Sc. Science. The implication of this situation is that future teachers of secondary school science will be drawn from the less bright science students. This can adversely affect the production of future science students including potential medical students.

Table 12 shows the sex distribution of Ghanaian medical students during the 1974 period. Of the total 501 students covered in the study sample, 89.9 per cent were males and only 10.1 per cent were females. A possible explanation is that female education is a recent phenomenon and those who get into the sixth forms tend to choose non-science subjects. I was informed by the Headmaster of Achimota School that girls are usually encouraged by their parents to do "what is expected of girls i.e. take home science and arts subjects". At the medical school admission level, however, no such discrimination exists. Admission procedure is based mainly on the academic performance of the student. In doubtful cases, the student's background is assessed to clear out any doubt regarding capacity to pursue "rigorous medical education".

The crucial variable in this analysis is the occupational background characteristics of the students' parents. This will help us to determine whether the socio-economic background of the parent is an important determinant in the intake of the Ghanaian medical school students. The author used Gustav Jahoda's scale of occupational grouping (Jahoda 1954: 360). In this analysis, he used the following variants of the occupational variable: Higher Profession, Lower Profession, Higher Commerce, Lower Commerce, Artisan and other manual workers, farmers, clerical and allied workers, miscellaneous and unclassified group. In the 1964 admission, 31.6 per cent were sons of farmers and 26.3 per cent were from the higher professions. In 1965, 23.3 per cent were from farming background and a significant 30 per cent were from unclassified background. In 1966, 25.9 per cent were from lower professional group, i.e. technical workers. In 1976, a similar situation persisted (25 per cent from lower profession), in 1968, farming: 22.2 per cent and higher professions: 28.9 per cent. In 1969, 22.2 per cent of the students were drawn from the farming and 22.2 per cent from lower professional categories. In 1971, 28.6 per cent came from the higher professional category. In 1972, 23.5 per cent were from the lower professional category. In 1973 and 1974, 27.1 and 27.4 per cent respectively were from the higher professional category. As seen in Table 13, the students' background is quite heterogeneous in terms of the

TABLE 11

"A" Level Performances of Students Admitted into the Ghana Medical School 1964–1974

Grade Year	A		B		C		D		E		Total	
	No.	%	No.	%	No.	%	No.	%	No.	%	No.	%
1964	11	9.7	—	—	5	1.6	22	7.2	1	6	—	3.0
1965	7	6.1	18	4.4	12	4.0	25	8.3	4	2.4	666	5.1
1966	9	7.9	15	3.7	14	4.5	11	3.7	12	7.4	61	4/7
1967	5	4.4	34	8.4	28	9.0	23	7.7	31	19.1	121	9.4
1968	4	3.7	29	7.2	20	6.5	40	13.3	25	15.5	118	9.2
1969	11	9.7	40	9.9	34	11.0	38	12.6	17	10.4	140	10.8
1970	6	5.1	37	9.2	38	12.5	37	12.3	24	15.0	142	11.0
1971	9	7.9	41	10.1	35	11.3	29	9.7	17	10.4	131	10.2
1972	17	14.9	71	17.6	49	15.9	20	6.7	6	3.8	163	12.8
1973	21	18.4	64	15.9	26	8.5	26	8.7	13	8.0	150	11.6
1974	14	12.2	55	13.6	47	15.2	29	9.7	12	7.4	157	12.2
Total	114	100	404	100	308	100	300	100	162	100	1288	100.0

Notes

(1) The above information represents 88.6 per cent of the student population between 1964–74 i.e. 57 students were without the necessary information.

(2) Students here offered 3 or 4 of the following subjects: (1) Chemistry (2) Biology (3) Physics

TABLE 12

**Male and Female Distribution of Students Admitted
into the Ghana Medical School 1964–1974**

Year	Male		Female		Total	
	No.	%	No.	%	No.	%
1964	35	92.1	3	7.9	38	100.0
1965	27	99.0	3	1.0	30	100.0
1966	21	77.8	6	22.2	27	100.0
1967	49	93.9	3	6.1	52	100.0
1968	44	97.8	1	2.2	45	100.0
1969	51	87.7	7	12.3	58	100.0
1970	46	86.8	7	13.2	53	100.0
1971	34	90.5	8	9.5	42	100.0
1972	49	89.3	6	10.7	55	100.0
1973	44	98.8	5	1.2	49	100.0
1974	49	93.9	3	6.1	52	100.0
Total	449	89.9	52	10.1	501	100.0

occupational groupings of their parents. In the final analysis, the observation is that medical students come from farming homes (20.2 per cent), from higher professions (19.8 per cent) and lower professional (16.7 per cent) backgrounds. It is also interesting to note that only 3.6 per cent of the student population had parents whose occupation had something to do with medicine at the time of entering the medical school. There is, however, a trend in favour of the higher professions and families in the higher socio-economic positions.

Discussion and Findings

In Canada and the United States, over 73 per cent of the physicians had fathers who were members of the three top classes and just over 17 per cent of the 1961 labour force were represented in these same classes.

The data of the social background of Euro-American medical students provide some indication of the social pre-conditioning which may sustain the medical student as he attempts to cope with the strains and

TABLE 13

Occupation of Parents of Students of the Ghana Medical School 1964–1974

Year	\	\	\	\	\	Occupational Group	\	\	\	\	\	\	\	\	\	\	Total	\
	1		2		3		4		5		6		7		8		Total	
	No.	%	No.	%	No.	%	No.	%	No.	%	No.	%	No.	%	No.	%	No.	%
1964	12	31.6	3	7.9	1	2.7	—	—	4	10.5	10	26.5	4	10.5	4	10.5	38	100.0
1965	7	23.3	3	10.0	—	—	1	3.4	4	13.3	3	10.0	3	10.0	9	30.0	30	100.0
1966	6	22.3	—	—	3	11.1	4	14.8	—	—	3	11.1	7	25.9	4	14.8	27	100.0
1967	11	21.2	4	7.7	4	7.7	2	4.0	4	7.7	4	7.7	13	25.0	10	19.0	52	100.0
1968	10	22.2	1	2.2	2	4.4	5	11.1	2	4.4	13	28.9	3	6.7	9	20.1	45	100.0
1969	14	24.1	4	6.9	4	6.9	6	10.1	4	6.9	12	20.2	10	17.0	4	6.9	58	100.0
1970	10	18.9	3	7.6	4	7.6	3	5.7	5	9.4	7	13.3	10	22.4	9	17.0	53	100.0
1971	6	14.3	2	—	—	—	2	4.7	8	19.1	12	28.6	6	14.3	6	14.3	42	100.0
1972	11	20.0	1	7.2	4	7.2	5	9.6	4	7.2	7	12.6	13	23.5	10	18.2	55	100.0
1973	7	13.3	3	—	—	—	6	11.2	4	7.1	14	27.6	8	15.3	10	19.4	49	100.0
1974	7	13.4	2	2.9	1	2.9	1	2.9	6	12.5	14	27.4	4	7.7	14	27.4	52	100.0
Total	101	20.2	26	4.7	23	4.7	35	6.9	45	8.9	99	19.8	83	16.7	89	17.8	501	100.0

Notes:

1. The Occupational Groups are: 1. Farming. 2. Artisan & Other Manual. 3. Clerical & Allied. 4. Higher Commerce. 5. Lower Commerce. 6. Higher Profession. 7. Lower Profession. 8. Miscellaneous & Unclassified.

2. See Gustav Jahoda, p.360 for explanation of Occupation Categories.

3. Only 3.6% of the student population had parents whose occupation had something to do with medicine at time of entering the medical school. Blishen, B. R. (1969: 34) *op. cit.*

4. 7.9% of the students had parents who belonged to the educational field (Lower Profession) at entry to the medical school e.g. (teachers, headmasters and mistresses, etc.)

engendered by the process of medical education. They also provide evidence to support Hall's claim that the ambition to study medicine is largely social in nature. That is to say, it is generated in and nourished by the groups to which the student belongs. The model of the father was a continuing example of what the future held. The family provided the financial means to support the ambition. Oswald Hall argues that admissions are made on the basis of technical proficiency but after that level of competence is reached, other factors take precedence over sheer proficiency. At this level, personal factors play a part in determining who will be accepted. However, personal traits are not really so important in determining admission as institutional acceptability. To the extent that hospitals have distinctive policies and unique histories, they tend to exclude doctors with certain backgrounds and to encourage others. Oswald Hall discusses the issues of inner fraternity of the medical profession. The indication is that as far as recruiting new members, allocating them for positions in the various medical institutions and securing clientele for them are concerned, there exists a set of controls exercised by a central core of the profession. This gives the main clue to the structure of the profession.

In Ghana, the analysis of occupational backgrounds of parents of medical students shows that social class determination is not an important factor. Students are recruited from all types of backgrounds. The picture shows that the majority of Ghanaian students do not come from the higher socio-economic sectors of the society. Many of the students' fathers were farmers, from miscellaneous backgrounds and from parents in the professional and administrative backgrounds. Amoa[10] in his thesis finds that "students whose fathers are farmers, petty traders and artisans make up about 68 per cent of the sample while only 32 per cent of the respondents' fathers are in white-collar jobs such as the civil service, business and medicine". The position is not very different from that of Jahoda's (1954) study. He found that a third of the fathers had farming background and that only a small minority had parents from the higher professions.

The reason why, in comparative terms, students who have wealthy parents tend to go into medicine in the Euro-American experience is because they pay for their university education and their parents are high among those most able and willing to pay. To be educated in medicine is an expensive enterprise. On the other hand, in Ghana since the late fifties, many students were virtually encouraged to take the opportunity to enter the free educational system from the secondary to the university levels.

This Ghanaian situation tends to explain why all types of students from different occupational backgrounds are recruited into the study of medicine and into other professions. It is possible to predict that in the near future socio-economic considerations will become an important issue because at present, only fairly rich parents can afford good secondary education for their children. Only well-to-do children will then be able to enter into medicine. But at present, the observation in the Ghanaian situation is different from the finding of the sociologists who have looked at the socialization process in the Euro-American experience and concluded that the social class factor is an important correlate in medical training.

There is yet another point. Lay people, physicians and sociologists alike, tend to subscribe to the view that one important fact in medical education is the development in the students a sense of professionalism;[11] that students are trained to be more "emotionally detached" and less "idealistic".[12] This view is based on the premise that for the most part medical students are trained to lose interest in their patients as people and to view patients as "mere embodiments of diseased entities."[13] The argument is that students are trained to be callous in the face of death and human suffering. Eron[14] for instance, discovered that when medical students were given tests on the "impersonal" and "humanitarian scale" they were found to score higher on the "impersonal" scale and to score lower on "humanitarian scale" as they advanced through the medical school. On the other hand, in the Ghanaian medical school, efforts are made to inject a civic sense into the medical education. Also a humanitarian attitude is installed into the medical students to help them develop human sensitivities in the practice of medicine.

It has been realized in Ghana that professionalism[15] also means the ability to be objective, to live up to the norm of detached concern[16] or to be interested in a patient without becoming emotionally involved,[17] to treat patients alike or to develop what Parsons terms affective neutrality and to shift from particularism to universalism.

This is fortunate, as in Ghana, the majority of the people live in rural and outlying settlements. The pattern of relationships in these areas is personal and particularistic and so an awareness of this fact is desirable in medical education.

Conclusion

In conclusion, the following propositions would seem to be warranted

(1) One's social class position has not been an important factor in the intake into the Ghana Medical School. However, as a result of the increasing cost of secondary education, in the very near future, the socio-economic background of the parent will be an important determinant in the intake of the Ghana Medical School, a reflection which should give food for thought.
(2) Medical students tend to be much younger than the average university students in the other faculties.

(3)   There is no clear crystalization of Ghanaian inner medical fraternity group controlling the type and nature of who gets admitted. The admission procedure is based solely on the academic performance of students.

(4)   The development of "concerned detachment" is necessary in medical education. It helps the professional to operate with objectivity and ensure that all types of patients will be treated fairly, while maintaining a humanitarian attitude.

REFERENCES

Bernard R. Blishen, *Doctors and Doctrines,* Toronto: University of Toronto Press, 1969, pp. 24–43.

Robert K. Merton, *Student Physician,* Cambridge, Mass: Harvard University Press, 1957.

J. R. Ellis, "Tomorrow's Doctors", *British Medical Journal,* Vol. 1, June 19, 1965, p.1573.

Oswald Hall, "The Stages of a Medical Career", *American Journal of Sociology,* Vol. 53, March 1948, pp. 327–36.

Ibid., p.329.

Howard S. Becker and Blanche Geer, "Medical Education", in Howard E. Freeman, *Handbook of Medical Sociology,* Englewood Cliffs: Prentice Hall Inc. 1963, pp. 169–189.

Gustav Johoda, "The Social Background of a West African Student Population", Part I. *British Journal of Sociology,* No. 5, 1954, p.355.

Margaret Peil, "Ghanaian University Students, The Broadening Base", *British Journal of Sociology,* Vol. 16, 1965, pp. 19–27.

Sakyi Awuku Amoa, *Ghanaian University Students: A Sociological Study of an Incipient Elite,* Unpublished M.A. Thesis, Department of Sociology, August 1969.

Ibid., p.30.

L. D. Eron, "Effect of Medical Education on Medical Students". *Journal of Medical Education,* Vol. 10, October 1955, pp. 559–66.

Howard S. Becker and Blande Geer, *op. cit.,* pp. 169–180.

T. Parsons, *Social System,* New York: Mac Co., 1958.

L. D. Eron, *op. cit.*

T. Parsons, *op. cit.*

Keene C. Fox, "Training for University" in R. K. Merton. *The Student Physician, op. cit.,* p.206.

Ibid., p.207.

Appendix

How the Research was Conducted

The author had the opportunity to travel in the company of Professor S. R. A. Dodu to Colombo, we discussed the desirability of researching into the background characteristics of Ghanaian medical students from 1964 to 1974.

On my return to Ghana, I approached Professor Dodu again and he gave me further assistance and encouragement. He suggested that I look into the existing records and interview some of the medical students and faculty.

With his co-operation, I appointed two research assistants to work on the project. The method was mainly examining records and doing some primary interviewing. The field work started in earnest in January 1975. Questions were framed to guide the research assistants. They were introduced to the rules of social investigation. I wrote letters of introduction for them to show to the appropriate authorities in case they were asked to declare their identity.

When they returned from the field, they came to discuss the data they had obtained. This interaction was necessary. At times, I went with them to see what they were doing. We were also able to interview a group of medical students and lecturers to find out their views and opinions on medical education. Information was obtained from diverse people.

The field work went smoothy. It took six months to complete. After the field work, we settled down to the processing of the field material. Statistical tables were framed and necessary calculations were made. From these statistical tables, the author extracted the information that formed the basis of this report.

Relevant literature in the area of medical education was read to see how others view medical education in other countries. This aspect of the work is a comparative one. Proper acknowledgement was given to all works cited in the reference notes.

2.   **Higher Education and Social Mobility in Ghana: The Case of the University of Ghana (Legon)[1]**

Dr. John Sinclair*

A university degree was the philosopher's stone. It transmitted a third-class clerk on one hundred and fifty a year into a Senior Civil Servant on five hundred and fifty, with a car and luxuriously furnished quarters at a nominal rent. And the disparity in salary and amenities did not even tell half the story. To occupy a "European post" was second only to actually being a European. It raised a man from the masses to the elite whose small talk at cocktail parties was: "How's the car behaving?" (Achebe 1960: 92).

Introduction

Apart from the novelist Achebe, a number of sociological writers have noted that access to most top occupational and social positions in the "new nations" of Africa is achieved through formal education; and for this reason, some of them have studied the characteristics of university or even secondary school students as potential members of the elites in these societies.[2] Of particular interest has been the geographical and socio-economic background of such students, for from these data, it can be assessed whether they are drawn equitably from all sections of the community, or whether they tend to be recruited mainly from the more privileged sections of the population. In other words, does the educational system operate as an effective vehicle in promoting social mobility between the different strata of society, or does it discriminate in favour of the children of higher status citizens perpetuating privilege from one generation to the next and thus, facilitating the crystallization of classes in Africa?

At least from an old-fashioned liberal point of view, there appears to be three main inter-related reasons why social mobility between the various strata in a society should be encouraged. Firstly, such mobility should promote the fullest utilization of the human resources of the society. There is no reason to believe that talent or ability is a monopoly of the members of any particular strata within society — indeed, they are likely to be dispersed among all strata. Thus, to ensure that the most capable individuals are able to rise to the key positions of leadership and responsibility within society from which they should be able to make their maximum contribution to the good of the community as a whole, social mobility must be encouraged.

---

* Former Lecturer, Department of Sociology, University of Cape Coast. Published by kind permission of the author.

A second reason for encouraging social mobility is to achieve social justice. All individuals should be offered equality of opportunity to reach the most responsible and highly-rewarded positions in society. This is especially so in societies such as the developing nations of Africa, which manifest a very high degree of inequality in the rewards given to individuals of different levels in their socio-economic hierarchies. The functional theory of social stratification attempts to justify such inequality in terms of the greater contributions to society as a whole by those in the more highly-rewarded positions, or in terms of the longer period of training which they require.[3] A minimum condition for such a justification to be valid, however, is that every individual should have a fair opportunity of reaching a position in society offering rewards commensurate with his ability and of obtaining the training necessary to quality for such a position; but it appears that in reality this condition is seldom met.

A third reason why social mobility may be considered desirable, especially by those opposed to radical political change is that social mobility may promote political stability. As long as members of the lower status sections of the population believe that society offers adequate opportunities for social mobility through education, they are unlikely to become a revolutionary "class-for-itself", to borrow Marxist terminology.[4] They will adhere to a naive form of the functional theory of social stratification, which suggests that the superior rewards of upper status individuals are a just return for their struggle and success in the educational system; and, perhaps more importantly, they may console themselves with the belief that either they themselves, if they are within what Plotnicov calls the "mobility zone", or otherwise their children, may achieve a similarly high level of rewards through future social mobility (Plotnicov 1970: 292–5). As W. Ofuatey-Kodjoe writes, with special reference to members of the working classes in Africa:

> . . . urban migrants are poor, not only in absolute terms but also in relation to their aspirations. Living as they do on the fringes of the ostentatious wealth of elite society and knowing of the poor origins of many of these wealthy people, they have hopes of realizing for themselves, the wealth and status which the politicians promised them would come after independence. The strategy that is often adopted in the quest for this social advancement is education either for oneself or his children . . . the pervasive naive belief in the ease of social mobility inhibits the formation of class consciousness on the part of the workers, and this is reflected in the ineffectiveness of their organizations (Ofuatey-Kodjoe 1975: 9).

In order words, members of the lower strata in African societies are not usually oriented towards improving their communal position through class action, but rather towards improving their personal position through individual social mobility.[5] In fact, such beliefs in the existence of opportunities for social mobility are perhaps not so naive as Ofuatey-Kodjoe suggests, for many elite members have their origins in quite humble homes.

Another more direct way by which social mobility reduces class solidarity among members of the lower socio-economic strata is by allowing their most able and qualified members to rise up and be incorporated into higher strata, with which they then identify. This has the effect of denuding the lower classes of their potentially most effective leadership and thus, contributes to defusing the possibility of overt class conflict. So social mobility plays an important part in the process of nation-building, not only because it promotes the fullest utilization of human resources for national development, but also because of its effect on the political stability and cohesion of society. It is, therefore, an important area of study for anyone who wishes to understand socio-economic and political developments in the new nations of Africa.

Strategy and Methods of Research

In this paper some of the results of a research project aimed at assessing the extent of opportunities for social mobility offered by the three universities in Ghana will be presented. By comparing the geographical and socio-economic origins of students with the composition of the total population in terms of the same characteristics, it is hoped to demonstrate whether opportunities for social mobility through higher education are equitably distributed throughout the population, or whether they are monopolized by the children of an already privileged elite. In other words, is Ghana a "meritocracy" in which the deal of equality of opportunity is closely approached, or are there signs that a more rigid type of class system is already crystalizing? Some preliminary results of this research, concerned particularly with students at Cape Coast, have already been published elsewhere (Sinclair 1975). This paper, therefore, will concentrate on the results obtained on students at the University of Ghana, Legon.

These results on Legon students are of special significance for two main reasons. Firstly, insofar as Legon forms the pinnacle of the Ghanaian educational system, it is potentially the most important gateway to upward social mobility and hence, the extent to which the recruitment of its students reveals either an open or closed pattern will be a particularly significant index of the degree to which equality of opportunity exists in contemporary Ghana. Secondary, most previous work in this field in Ghana has been done at Legon, which allows for effective comparisons of mobility rates at different points in time and thus, an assessment of whether opportunities for mobility are increasing or decreasing.[6] This is of particular interest in the present study, especially as previous writers have shown a lack of agreement on the matter. For example, Margaret Peil, on the basis of a comparison of students at Legon in 1964 with those who were there a decade earlier, came to the conclusion that there is "a long term trend toward a student body more representative of the population as a whole (Peil 1965: 23). Bibby, however, questioned the statistical adequacy of the evidence on which Peil based her results suggesting that the alleged trend was "either illusory or transitory" (Bibby 1973: 371). Hurd and Johnson also take a much less optimistic view of the situation than Peil, believing that in Ghana, the balance of educational opportunity is swinging in favour of the children of the more privileged sections of the population, while the children of the less privileged will find it increasingly difficult to obtain university education and thereby enter the elite (Hurd and Johnson 1967: 77–79). The results presented in this paper should provide up-to-date evidence to help in reassessing these arguments.

Before proceeding further, however, it is necessary to take note of the fact that the present study, like most previous researches in the field, is of limited generality: it does not tell us about the overall pattern of social mobility in the society as a whole, but only about opportunities for upward social mobility through higher education. It is assumed that higher education is the most important means of access to the elite positions within society; but this remains an assumption which is never actually tested in the present type of research. In fact, there are other means of social mobility — e.g. through success in business, politics, or the armed services — and graduates obviously have differential success in achieving the highest prized positions after leaving university; but these aspects of mobility are neglected in the present study. In addition, concentration on university students obviously tells us mainly about upward mobility, though, as Fox and Miller point out, "downward mobility may be indicative of social fluidity than upward mobility" (Fox and Miller 1967: 575). But until a more comprehensive survey of social mobility can be carried out, giving a "mobility profile" of Ghanaian society as a whole, studies of university students are likely to remain our best indication of the extent of opportunities for social mobility.

The data on students required for this study were obtained from their personal files compiled by the University Registry, and in particular, from the University application forms included in these files. It seems likely that higher quality data could have been obtained from interviews or questionnaires administered directly to students. For example, when using interviews and questionnaires, it is possible to include questions which should obtain the exact information required, while in using files, it is necessary to accept the data available in them, which is not always ideal.[7] In addition, the data to be found in application forms may be distorted by the candidates' desire to present as favourable an impression of themselves as possible.

Considering the advantages of interviews and questionnaires, it was decided to collect the basic data from the student files because of the cheapness, efficiency and convenience of this method in gathering information on a large number of cases. Thus, it was possible for one well-trained research assistant to collect information on nearly all undergraduates at Legon, recording these data directly onto pre-coded sheets in a form suitable for punching straight onto I.B.M. cards for computer processing. This not only reduces the costs and need for elaborate supervision inherent in large scale social surveys, but also helps eliminate inaccuracies which might have resulted from employing a large number of less well-qualified assistants for interviewing and coding, or by the respondents' misuderstanding of the questions in a self-administered questionnaire.

Another advantage of the files method of data collection is that it facilitates longitudinal studies requiring the comparison of past students with present students, for data on past students are also available in the files, while to obtain comparable data on them by means of interviews or questionnaires would be a difficult, if not totally impracticable, exercise. In fact, the records on past students were not used in the present study, but as Peil's data on 1963 Legon students were also collected from files, they provided an ideal point of comparison with those on 1973/74 students collected in this survey (Peil 1965). As explained above, such longitudinal comparison forms an important aspect of the present research project.

Finally, it may be noted that the files method allows data to be collected without troubling the respondents, and this not only saves inconveniencing them, but also ensures that a relatively complete sample is obtained, for it reduces the various problems of non-response encountered when administering interviews and questionnaires.[8] Thus, in the present study, information was obtained on 96 per cent of the 1,800 undergraduates at Legon during the 1973/74 academic session.[9] As the main interest in the research project is in the opportunities for social mobility available to young Ghanaians, the 46 non-Ghanaian students in the sample have been excluded; and hence subsequent analysis in this paper will be based on a sample of 1,680 of the Ghanaian undergraduates at Legon.

The Geographical and Socio-economic Background of Students at Legon

Perhaps the most important question raised in this paper concerns the extent to which there is equality of opportunity for young people of differing geographical and socio-economic backgrounds to enter university and thus, achieve the kind of social mobility which results from success in higher education. As indices of the students' geographical and socio-economic background, special attention will be paid to their regions of birth, the sizes of their places of birth in terms of number of inhabitants and the types of occupation practised by their guardians. In Tables 14, 15 and 16 these indices are used to compare the characteristics of students at Legon

TABLE 14*

Sex by Region of Birth of Ghanaian Undergraduates at Legon, Compared with the Distribution of the Total Population

Region of Birth	Sex		Total	Ghana Total**
	Males	Females		
	%	%	%	%
Western	6.6	8.8	6.9	9.0
Central	9.4	11.0	9.6	10.4
Greater Accra	14.5	33.0	17.0	9.9
Eastern	19.0	17.2	18.8	14.7
Volta	16.9	7.0	15.5	11.1
Ashanti	20.4	14.1	19.5	17.3
Brong-Ahafo	4.0	2.2	3.8	9.0
Northern	1.8	0.9	1.7	8.5
Upper	4.3	0.9	3.9	10.1
Outside Ghana or don't know	3.2	4.8	3.4	—
Total %	100.1	99.9	100.1	100.0
No.	1453	227	1680	8,559,313

Notes
* Tables 14–23 refer to Tables 1–10 in the original article.
**Derived from *1970 Population Census of Ghana*.

with the characteristics of the total population in an attempt to elucidate the extent to which there is openness of access to university education in Ghana.

A glance at these Tables reveals that Legon students are in fact drawn from all sections of the population; but comparison of students from various types of background with the characteristics of the total population of Ghana shows a considerable degree of inequality of entering university. Table 14, for example, makes it clear that students are drawn from all regions, sometimes, as in the cases of those from the Western, Central, and Ashanti Regions in proportions quite similar to what would be expected from the proportions the inhabitants of these regions form of the total population. Nevertheless, certain anomalies do exist. Greater Accra and the Volta Region, for example, are over-represented in terms of the numbers of students they send to Legon. Brong-Ahafo and the Northern

TABLE 15

Sex by Size of Place of Birth for Ghanaian Undergraduates at Legon, Compared with the Distribution of the Total Population

Size of Place of Birth	Sex		Total	Ghana Total**
	Males	Females		
	%	%	%	%
Over 100,000	24.8	51.1	28.3	11.0
10,000–99,999	22.8	27.8	23.5	11.5
5,000–9,999	13.9	6.2	12.9	6.5
2,000–4,999	15.2	6.6	14.0	11.2
Under 2,000	18.2	3.1	16.2	59.9
Outside Ghana, or don't know	5.0	5.3	5.1	—
Total %	99.9	100.1	100.0	100.1
No.	1,435	227	1,680	8,559,313

**Derived from the 1970 *Population Census of Ghana*.

and Upper Regions, on the other hand, are under-represented, for, though they together contain over one quarter of the total population of Ghana, they provide only about one tenth of the students at Legon.

It also appears that young people born in the larger towns have a much better chance of entering university than those from smaller settlements. Thus, as can be seen from Table 15, over half of the Legon undergraduates had been born in towns with 10,000 or more inhabitants, though less than one quarter of the population live in such towns. Some of this effect may result from students' mothers who, though actually living in villages, travelled to hospitals in larger towns to give birth. Probably, this is not crucial in explaining the pattern, however, for the few mothers who are likely to have done this, especially at the time when the students were born, and in any case, the effect is likely to have been balanced by a movement of women in the reverse direction, returning from towns to their home villages to give birth.[10]

These quite substantial variations in geographical terms may be explained largely by the uneven diffusion of elementary and secondary education throughout the country, for educational institutions came first to the towns of the coastal area and only later spread to other parts of Ghana. Even today, educational facilities, particularly at the higher levels, are not

TABLE 16

Sex by Occupational Status of the Next-of-kin of Ghanaian Undergraduate at Legon, Compared with the Occupational Distribution of all Employed Males Aged 15 and Over

Occupational Status	Sex		Total	Ghana Total**
	Males	*Females*		
	%	%	%	%
Professional, administrative, managerial	17.6	37.2	20.1	1.3
Lower professional and executive	16.7	23.5	17.5	4.1
Clerical and supervisory	12.9	11.7	12.8	5.3
Higher commercial	6.9	9.2	7.2	1.0
Lower commercial	10.1	5.6	9.5	2.9
Skilled manual	2.8	2.0	2.7	11.5
Semi-skilled	3.2	1.0	2.9	8.7
Unskilled manual	0.5	—	0.4	8.1
Agricultural and related activities	29.2	9.7	26.8	60.1
Total %	99.9	100.1	99.9	100.0
Total No.	1,369	196	1,565	1,706,665
Excluded from analyses	84	31	115	11,163

Note:
(a) Unpublished figures from the 1970 *Population Census of Ghana,* by courtesy of the Government Statistician.
(b) There are many non-workers, such as housewives and students, and those whose occupations were unknown. For a more detailed breakdown of the occupational classification, see note 12.

evenly distributed throughout the country resulting in potential students from the more remote areas being at a considerable disadvantage in obtaining the basic education necessary to qualify for university entrance.

In addition, the desire of parents to send their children to school should not be taken as axiomatic: it is another independent variable which may be a cause of different rates of school attendance in different areas.

As Philip Foster points out, in developing societies formal education is not usually desired as an end in itself, but rather because of the material benefits which it may confer. Thus, in Ghana the popular demand for education only manifests itself after certain economic developments provided lucrative employment opportunities for the educated (Foster 1965: 124–37). In this case, it is possible that the high proportion of students from the southern parts of the country in general, and from the larger towns in particular results from a greater appreciation of the value of education in these more developed areas.

This latter factor, however, is probably of only marginal significance today. As Hurd and Johnson point out, the Volta Region is underdeveloped economically, but nevertheless its people are over-represented in most institutions of higher education (Hurd and Johnson 1967: 66). This may be partly attributed to the long tradition of education in the Region, which suggests that, even in the absence of local economic development, the existence of educational facilities may create its own demand for more education. In fact, it is partly the lack of economic opportunities in their own area which forces inhabitants of the Volta Region to seek an education to qualify themselves for occupational positions in other parts of Ghana. So, though they may still be motivated by the desire to take advantage of occupational opportunities, as Forster suggests, such opportunities need not necessary be in their own part of the country to create a desire for education.

In general, it would seem unlikely that in contemporary Ghana, many parents are unaware of the benefits of education. If they do not send their children to school, it is probably because of economic constraints rather than because they do not favour education.[11] It would seem likely that the differences in ability of parents to pay school fees may partly explain the geographical variations in school attendance, for better-off parents tend to live in towns and their presence is reflected in the higher proportion of urban children entering university.

The effect of socio-economic background in influencing a young person's chances of entering university is clearly evident in Table 16, which compares the occupational statuses of the next-of-kin of undergraduates at Legon with the occupational statuses of all employed males in Ghana.[12] This shows that students are much more likely to come from homes of high socio-economic status than would be expected from the number of such homes in the society. Thus, about half of all undergraduates have other white collar occupations, though only about one tenth of all male workers in Ghana are in such occupation; and the wards of businessmen and traders also appear overrepresented among Legon students.[13] The wards of farmers and fishermen, on the other hand, are found less than half as often as would be expected from the proportion of such workers in the total population. In addition, as Hurd and Johnson suggest, many of these students may be the children of a relatively small number of prosperous agricultural entrepreneurs, while the children of small peasants and the rural proletariat have a very poor chance of obtaining a university education (Hurd and Johnson 1967: 71–3). The most severely under-represented group in the student population appears to be the wards of manual workers — and particularly of unskilled manual workers — for they are found less than one quarter as often as would be expected. This seems to confirm the verdict of earlier research that the children of the urban proletariat are the most underprivileged section of society (e.g. Hurd and Johnson 1967: 73; Foster 1968: 112).

Most obviously, such variation in opportunities of obtaining a university education between young people of differing socio-economic backgrounds results from differences in the ability of their parents to afford the cost of their pre-university education. Secondary education in particular is relatively expensive in Ghana and is, therefore, usually beyond the reach of students with poor parents. Costs at the elementary level, on the other hand, are fairly low; but so are the educational standards in the normal government schools. The child whose parents can afford to give him the superior elementary education available in the so-called "international schools" will have a considerably enhanced chance of qualifying for entry into higher level institutions.[14] In addition, poor parents may find it difficult to forgo the economic contributions which their children may make to the upkeep of the family if they enter gainful employment rather than continue at school.

It should also be recognized that a child's educational progress and, hence, his subsequent chances of entering university may be influenced by his socio-cultural background, with children from more "sophisticated" backgrounds having an educational advantage over those from illiterate homes. For example, the child whose parents have Western education may benefit from the use of the English language in the home, which may ease his transition to the use of English in the classroom; and also, his parents may be able to coach him in his school work, a possibility which hardly exists in the illiterate home. In addition, children from well-off homes may possess several other educational advantages, such as quiet places to study and access to various educational media, such as books, magazines, radio and television. Taken together, these various factors have a cumulative effect in favouring children from well-off homes, giving them a considerable advantage over those from poorer homes in obtaining the university education which would qualify them for membership of the socio-economic elite.

Sex and Differential Educational Opportunities

Not only may inequalities of educational opportunity within Ghanaian society be illustrated by comparing the characteristics of students with those of the total population, but also by looking at variations within the student population itself. The most obvious of these variations is that between male and female students. As can be seen by re-examining Table 14, 15 and 16, Ghanaian females have a much poorer chance than their male counterparts of entering university, for female students form only about one seventh of all students at Legon. This may be attributed to two main factors; firstly, the generally lower levels of educational and occupational aspirations among females compared with males, based presumably on the rather inferior social roles which male-dominated society assigns them;[15] and secondly, the priority which is usually given to male education, especially when a family's resources are insufficient to allow all its children to be sent to school. Parents consider the education of a son a better investment than that of a daughter, a point which is again related to the fact that males generally occupy the more highly rewarded positions in society.[16]

The degree of priority given to the education of males varies according to the resources available to the parents. Well-off parents will be able to pay for the education of both their sons and daughters, while less well-off parents may be able to afford to send only their sons to school. As a result, female students are even more likely than their male counterparts to come from geographically and socially privileged backgrounds. In regional terms, for example, female students are much more likely than male students to come from Greater Accra, indicating that Accra parents are in a better position than those in other parts of the country to send not only their sons to school, but also many of their daughters. Males and females from the Western, Central and Eastern Regions are represented roughly in the proportions which would be expected from their numbers in the student population as a whole, but among students from all other regions, the proportions of females are particularly low, indicating the concentration on male education in these areas of scarce economic and social resources. Similarly, female students are more likely than males to come from the larger towns. About half of all females were born in the three towns in Ghana with more than 100,000 inhabitants (i.e. Accra, Kumasi, and Sekondi-Takoradi) compared with only one quarter of male students. On the other hand, female students are particularly unlikely to come from the smaller villages, for most villagers exhaust their meagre financial resources by sending only a few of their sons to school.

In a similar way, female educational opportunities are even more concentrated among the children of high status parents than those of males. Thus, three fifths of female undergraduates at Legon had next-of-kin in professional, administrative, managerial and executive occupations, compared with only one third of male undergraduates, while the proportion of females with next-of-kin in farming, fishing and manual occupations was only about one third of males. To summarize the position, selectivity in terms of social and geographical background is even more marked among females than among males, which reflects not only the various causes of educational inequality discussed in the last section, but also the priority given to the education of males, especially in the poorer sections of society. A balanced educational policy for Ghana should seek to encourage female education, but it would have to make sure that the benefits of such encouragement do not go solely to the daughters of the already privileged upper and middle classes but also reach the children of the presently depressed classes of poor farmers and manual workers.

Pre-university Educational and Occupational Experience of Legon Undergraduates

The educational disadvantaged position of young people from lower status homes is manifest not only in their relative under-representation in the student population at Legon. It is also demonstrated by the fact that students from such homes who do actually manage to reach university appear to have experienced greater difficulty in doing so than their counterparts from better-off backgrounds. For example, students from less privileged backgrounds are less likely than others to have come straight to university by the direct route through secondary school. Instead, they are more likely to have proceeded from elementary school to teacher training college and to have worked for some time, particularly as teachers, before entering university.

This pattern of inequality between students of differing geographical and socio-economic backgrounds in terms of their pre-university experience can be seen clearly from Tables 17 and 18. From these tables, it is apparent that students from more privileged backgrounds — i.e. from larger towns and from homes of higher socio-economic status — are younger than those from less privileged backgrounds, which is presumably because they have usually entered university straight from secondary school. The latter, on the other hand, are less likely to have attended secondary school, but are more likely to have been at teacher training college and to have worked for some time before coming to university. Two examples will serve to emphasize the point. In the first place, as can be seen from Table 17 three fifths of undergraduates born in towns with more than 100,000 inhabitants were 22 years of age or under, compared with only about one fifth of those from villages with fewer than 2,000 people. Secondly, while about half of the wards of farmers and manual workers had been employed for some time before coming to university, as shown in Table 18, this was true to none of the 22 wards of medical doctors in the student population and also of only 5 per cent of the wards' of business managers, 6 per cent of the wards of lawyers and 7 per cent of the wards of the larger type of private businessmen.

TABLE 17

Size of Birthplace by Pre-university Experience of Ghanaian Undergraduates at Legon

Size of Birthplace	Proportion of Legon Students who:–				
	are aged 22 and under	have attended sec. school	have attended Form VI	have attended train. coll.	have had previous employ.
	%	%	%	%	%
Over 100,000	61.7	97.7	94.2	3.6	14.9
10,000–99,999	48.5	92.1	87.0	11.5	27.3
5,000–9,999	42.0	86.9	82.2	17.8	31.0
2,000–4,999	31.3	78.0	62.5	26.3	43.3
Under 2,000	22.6	71.1	64.7	35.0	53.4
All Students	44.5	87.5	81.7	16.0	30.6
No. of cases	735	1,447	277	265	506
Total	1,652	1,654	339	1,654	1,651
Excluded from analysis	28	26	2	26 ᵇ	29

Notes: Notes (a), (b) and (d) also apply to Tables 18 and 19.
a.   At the end of 1973.
b.   Figures for this are only available for a 20 per cent sub-sample of Legon students.
c.   Data for students who the size of their birth place is unknown have been included in this total, though they have been excluded from the rest of the Table.
d.   These are mainly cases in which the inclusion of the students in the selected category was problamatic (e.g. students whose ages are

The main causes of these variations are not hard to guess. Probably, the most important one is the fact that less well-off guardians are unable to afford to send their wards to secondary school and so the latter have to work their own way to university. It is also possible that children from less privileged homes do less well in the Common Entrance Examination which selects students for secondary school, either because their elementary schools are inferior to those attended by children from better-off homes, or because their socio-cultural backgrounds adversely affect their academic performance; and as a result, they fail to gain admission

TABLE 18

Occupational Status of Next-of-kin by Pre-university Experience of Ghanaian Undergraduates at Legon

Occupational status of next-of-kin	Proportion of Legon Students who:-				
	are aged 22 and under	have attended sec. school	have attended Form VI	have attended train. coll.	have had previous employ.
	%	%	%	%	%
Professional, administrative, managerial	64.3	98.1	96.7	2.9	13.5
Professional and executive	51.3	93.8	91.4	8.1	21.2
Clerical and supervisory	45.5	90.5	87.1	11.6	24.9
Higher Commercial	57.1	99.1	91.7	0.9	4.5
Lower Commercial	37.0	88.5	82.9	17.6	38.8
Manual	27.1	74.5	61.1	27.7	47.4
Agric. & related activities	25.1	72.1	65.1	35.0	52.7
All Students	44.5	87.5	81.7	16.0	30.7
No. of cases	735	1,447	277	265	506
Total	1,652	1,654	339	1,654	1,651
Excluded from analysis	28	26	2	26	[b] 29

Note
c.   Data for students who had next-of-kin who were non-workers or whose occupations were unknown have been included in this total, though they have been excluded from the rest of the Table.

to secondary schools. As they mature, however, their underlying intelligence asserts itself — or their strenuous efforts at last pay off — and they are eventually able to qualify for university by private study. But many of their contemporaries, though they may be equally capable of academic work, are less successful, as can be seen from the gross under-representation at university of students from under-privileged homes.

As seen in the above examples, there appears to be a fairly close parallel between the representation of students from different types of geographical and socio-economic backgrounds in the students populations and the degree of difficulty which students from these various backgrounds experience in actually reaching university. This also seems to be generally the case when we compare the relative representation at university and the pre-university experience of students born in different regions. For example, students born in Greater Accra are not only greatly over-represented at Legon, but are also particularly likely to have come straight from secondary school, as can be seen from Table 19, while the reverse is true of students from Brong-Ahafo. The Western, Central, Eastern and Ashanti Regions occupy intermediate positions on both scales. But the Volta, Northern and Upper Regions appear to offer partial exceptions to this rule of parallelism between the extent of representation of students from different regions and their pre-university experience.

The Volta Region is more obviously exceptional in this respect. As was pointed out above, students born in the Volta Region are over-represented at Legon; but yet they appear to have experienced greater difficulty than students from any other region in reaching university. For example, they are older on average than students from all other regions; and they are also less likely to have attended secondary school, particularly to sixth form and are more likely to have attended training college. After students born in Brong-Ahafo, they are most likely to have been employed before coming to university. In addition, as can be seen by looking back to Table 14, a relatively small proportion of students from Volta Region are females, which is another sign that, despite its over-representation at Legon, the Volta Region is essentially an under-privileged area. In fact, this supports the earlier contention that the high proportion of Volta Region students at Legon is not a sign of the Region's prosperity, but rather reflects an exceptionally high demand for education, probably generated by the early provision of elementary schooling, the lack of alternative employment opportunities for uneducated people in the Region, and perhaps by the nature of the Ewe people themselves.

The pattern displayed by students from the Northern and Upper Regions is also anomalous though less markedly so than that of the Volta Region. The under-privileged position of students from these Regions is shown not only in their under-representation at Legon, but also in their concentration in the older age categories and the relatively high proportion of them who were employed before coming to University. But, on the other hand, the proportion of them who attended secondary school, even to sixth form, is second only to Greater Accra. This is presumably a result of the policy aimed at encouraging the spread of education in the North of

TABLE 19

Region of Birth by Pre-university Experience of Ghanaian Undergraduates at Legon

	Proportion of Legon Students who:–				
Region of Birth	*are aged 22 and under*	*have attended sec. school*	*have attended Form VI*	*have attended train. coll.*	*have had previous employ.*
	%	%	%	%	%
Greater Accra	62.3	96.8	90.6	4.6	17.7
Western and Central	47.6	88.8	80.4	14.5	27.8
Eastern	40.8	86.9	81.7	17.3	28.9
Ashanti	44.9	87.6	82.1	16.1	27.4
Volta	30.4	77.2	69.4	26.8	46.3
Brong Ahafo	34.4	79.4	80.0	25.4	47.5
Northern and Upper	34.1	89.0	83.3	18.7	45.6
All Students	44.5	87.5	81.7	16.0	30.6
No. of cases	735	1,447	277	265	506
Total	1,652	1,654	339	1,654	1,651
Excluded from analysis	28	26	2	26	29

Note
c.   Data for students whose region of birth was unknown have been included in this total, though they have been excluded from the rest of the Table.

Ghana, which provides free education for students from the Northern and Upper Regions and which allows promising students from teacher training colleges to enter sixth forms directly without first passing through the lower forms of secondary school. This policy may be judged a partial success, for the proportion of students from the Northern and Upper Regions has risen slightly since previous studies; but it should be noted that they are still the most under-represented section of the population.[18]

In general, it may be noted that, though about four fifths of undegraduates enter Legon directly from the sixth forms of secondary schools, an important minority, especially of those from under-privileged backgrounds, have had no secondary education before coming to university. Teacher training and private study provide a "backdoor" to university for a relatively high proportion of students from poor homes and hence, this route is highly significant for the rate of upward social mobility in Ghana. If any educational reform is contemplated which would likely cut down on the use of this "backdoor", it would be advisable to consider the implications of this for social mobility and also the possible socio-political consequences of a significant reduction in the rate of upward social mobility.

Inter-Faculty Variations

One policy which may have the effect of reducing opportunities for entry into university without secondary education is the government's attempt to progressively concentrate undergraduates in subject areas which are assumed to make specially significant contributions to national economic development, such as pure science, medicine, agriculture and engineering. It is especially difficult for students without secondary education to qualify in these subjects, and, as was seen in the last section, such students tend to come from lower status homes. They lack access to the laboratories and equipment required for studying science to A-level standard, and in addition, elementary schools and training colleges have provided them with no basic training in science on which they could build. It is also true that good science teachers and facilities tend to be concentrated in the elite secondary schools and if children of high status parents manage to gain entry into these in disproportionate numbers, then this will again increase their chances of qualifying to study science-based subjects at university relative to those from less privileged backgrounds.[19]

It is also possible that as science subjects, together with law, are probably the most prestigious at Ghanaian universities the competition to enter them may be most keen and candidates from less privileged family and educational backgrounds may find it difficult to reach the standards set by their counterparts from more favoured backgrounds.[20] It may, therefore, be predicted that the latter will be over-represented relative to the former in the more prestigious faculties at Legon, such as science, medicine and law, while the reverse will be true in the less pretigious faculties.

This prediction appears to be at least partially supported by the evidence available in Tables 20 and 21. There is of course considerable overlap in the composition of faculties but there is some tendency for students in the faculties of science, medicine and law to come from homes which are more privileged in geographical and socio-economic terms than students in the faculties of Agriculture, Arts, Economics and Administration. For example, while over two fifths of students in Science and Medicine were born in the three towns in Ghana with more than 100,000 inhabitants,

TABLE 20

Size of Place of Birth of Ghanaian Undergraduates at Legon by their Faculty of Study

Size of Place of Birth	Faculty						Total
	Science	Medicine	Law	Agric.	Arts*	Adm.	
100,000 and over	42.3	41.3	36.3	27.9	25.0	22.9	29.8
100,000–99,999	28.1	24.9	26.3	27.9	24.2	22.3	24.8
5,000–9,999	8.9	10.7	12.5	18.3	13.6	18.6	13.5
2,000–4,999	7.4	11.0	13.8	10.6	17.5	17.0	14.8
Under 2,000	13.3	12.1	11.3	15.4	19.7	19.1	17.1
Total %	99.9	100.0	100.2	100.1	100.0	99.9	100.0
No.	135	281	80	104	807	188	1,595
Excluded from analysis	9	15	4	5	42	10	85

* Excludes 30 students from the Faculty of Economics, which are being phased out at the time of the study.

TABLE 21

Occupational Statuses of Fathers and Next-of-kin of Ghanaian Undergraduates at Legon by their Faculty of Study

Occupational Status of	Faculty						Total
	Science	Medicine	Law	Agric.	Arts*	Adm.	
Professional, Adm. managerial	23.5	24.2	31.6	21.4	17.2	17.8	20.1
Lower professional and executive	20.5	21.0	15.2	14.6	15.8	20.0	17.5
Clerical and supervisory	18.2	11.7	15.2	17.5	10.8	15.6	12.8
Higher Commercial	10.6	9.6	7.6	5.8	6.2	6.1	7.2
Lower Commercial	7.6	10.7	3.8	8.7	9.7	11.1	9.5
Manual	6.1	3.9	3.8	5.8	8.0	2.8	6.1
Agric. and related activities	13.6	18.9	22.8	26.2	32.3	26.7	26.8
Total %	100.1	100.0	100.0	100.0	100.0	100.1	100.0
Total No.	132	281	79	103	790	180	1,565
Excluded from analysis	12	15	5	6	59	18	115

* Includes 30 students from the Faculty of Economics, which was being phased out at the time of the study.

this was true of only between one fifth and one quarter of students in Arts, Economics and Administration. And less than one quarter of students in Science and Medicine had next-of-kin in agricultural and manual occupations compared with about two fifths of students in the faculties of Arts and Economics. Agriculture seems to occupy an intermediate position, perhaps because it is subject to contradictory influences: on the one hand, it is like the high status subjects in so far as its entry qualifications are mainly science-based, but on the other hand it is likely to appeal particularly to students from the rural areas who are likely to come mainly from homes of lower than average socio-economic status.

Of course, it may be admitted that though most of these variations are fairly marginal yet they may have some effect on opportunities for social mobility. This would occur at two main levels. Firstly, in so far as students without secondary education, who come mainly from lower status backgrounds, find it difficult to enter the faculties of Science, Medicine and Law, this reduces the opportunity for them to be socially mobile below what it would have been if all places at university were as accessible to them as those in the faculties of Arts, Economics and Administration. Secondly, it seems that the faculties of Medicine, Law, and perhaps Science are the most prestigious at Legon, or at least lead to the most pretigious occupations. If those from lower status backgrounds find it difficult to enter these faculties, then this will act as a constraint on their future mobility, for after graduation they will be unable to enter the highest status occupations. Instead, they will be mainly confined to the fields of secondary school teaching and administration which, probably, not only have less prestige than careers in medicine, law and pure science, but may also offer fewer promotion opportunities for, they will most rapidly become saturated with graduate employees.

Of course this threat to social mobility is not particularly severe at the present time, for the majority of students are still reading the Arts and Social Science subjects which draw most heavily on those from lower status homes. But if the kind of policy recently proposed by the National Council for Higher Education (which would force students in the so-called non-priority subjects to pay their own fees and find their own food and accommodation) were to be implemented, then this might have a serious effect in reducing the rate of upward social mobility through higher education, both by drastically reducing the number of the students in those faculties which most encourage social mobility and by limiting access to those places to students who can afford to pay the not inconsiderable fees.[21] Before such an inequitable policy is embarked upon, therefore, steps should be taken to reform the pre-university educational system so that all potential students have an equal chance of entering the privleged priority areas, irrespective of their socio-economic backgrounds.[22]

The Logitudinal Trend in Upward Social Mobility through Higher Education

The final topic to be discussed concerns the extent to which patterns of social mobility have been changing over time, or, more particularly, the extent to which opportunities for upward social mobility through university education has been increasing or decreasing. The existence of inequalities of educational opportunity has been consistently emphasized in this paper, but it should be realized that there are other ways of interpreting these statistics. Clignet and Foster, for example, in looking at similar statistics on secondary school pupils in Ghana and the Ivory Coast, choose to emphasize the relatively high proportion who do actually come from humble homes and the fluidity of the system of social status which this implies. In fact, an investigator's assessment of the situation will depend on which measures of mobility and standards of comparison he uses and, as Clignet and Foster point out, these in turn may be influenced by his "ideological stance" (Clignet and Foster 1966: 202). One way round this problem of subjectivity in assessing rates of social mobility is to concentrate on trends in mobility over a period of time, for, though because of the lack of any definitive "benchmarks" it may be impossible to specify that rates of mobility at a particular point in time are either high or low, it should at least be possible to decide whether they are becoming higher or lower.[23] Such longitudinal studies of trends in mobility in West Africa are of particular interest because, as explained in the introduction, previous research in this area has been inconclusive.

The best-known study of longitudinal trends in recruitment to the undergraduate population in Ghana is probably that of Peil, which suggests a "broadening base" of students in socio-economic terms (Peil 1965). But when the results of the present study are compared with those of Peil, as in Table 22 a rather different picture emerges, suggesting that since Peil's research was conducted in 1963, students at Legon have been increasingly drawn from homes of higher rather than lower socio-economic status. Thus, in the ten years after Peil's study, the proportion of students with next-of-kin in professional, administrative, managerial, executive and higher commercial occupations has more than doubled, while the proportion with next-of-kin in agricultural and manual occupations has fallen by about one third.

Of course, it is possible that this change has resulted from a shift in the occupational distribution of the total labour force, as an increasing proportion of workers are employed in higher status occupations and a decreasing proportion in agricultural and manual employment. For this hypothesis to be examined, Table 22 includes figures comparing the occupational distribution of all employed males aged 15 years and over in 1960 and 1970. Even a cursory examination of these figures shows that

TABLE 22

Occupational Statuses of Fathers and Next-on-kin of Undergraduates at Legon in 1953, 1963, and 1973 with the Occupational Distribution of all Employed Males in 1960 and 1970, and Selectivity Indices for 1960s and 1970s

Occupational Statuses of Fathers and Next-of-kin	Next-of-kin of Undergraduates [a]			All Employed Males [b]		Selectivity Indices [c]	
	1953	1963	1973	1960	1970	1960s	1970s
Professional & Adm.	9.6	8.4	17.3	1.0	1.3	8.4	13.4
Lower Prof. & Exe.	17.4	10.2	19.1	2.5	4.1	4.1	4.7
Clerical & Sup.	12.8	10.2	6.4	3.4	5.3	3.0	1.2
Higher Comm. & Manag.	6.8	3.6	10.9	0.6	1.0	6.0	10.9
Lower Commercial	16.1	14.4	10.4	3.7	2.9	3.9	3.6
Manual	8.3	11.4	6.7	26.0	25.3	0.4	0.3
Agric. & related actv.	28.9	41.9	29.2	62.7	60.1	0.7	0.5
Total %	99.9	100.1	100.0	99.9	100.0	—	—
No.	384	167	1,436	1,559,956	1,706,665	—	—
Excluded from analysis	47	14	244	8,009	11,163	—	—

Notes:

a. The data for 1953 are drawn from Jahoda (1954: 360) and those for 1963 from Peil (1965: 23). They have been recalculated so as to exclude the miscellaneous category from the comparison. Note that Jahoda's figures give father's occupations, while Peil's give the occupations of next-of-kin, as in the present study. The 1973 figures are from the present study, but they have been recalculated so as to make them more comparable with the previous studies. In particular, managers have been reallocated from the professional to the higher commercial category, while soldiers, policemen and ungraded civil servants have been excluded from the analysis.

b. The 1960 figures are from the *Population Census of Ghana, Vol/ 4*, while those in 1970 are unpublished figures kindly made available by the Government Statistician.

c. Selectivity indices are calculated by dividing the proportion of a group in the sample (e.g. the proportion of those with next-of-kin in professional and administration occupations) by its proportion in the total population.

there has been relatively little change in the occupational distribution during this ten-year period, suggesting that this cannot account for the changing socio-economic background of university students. But the point is made more rigorously by the selectivity indices which are also included in Table 22. These indices are calculated by dividing the proportion of students from a given type of socio-economic background by the proportion of this same group in the total population and they, therefore, give a general idea of the extent to which the group exceeds or falls below its expected quota in the student population. The increased dispersion or gradient of the selectivity indices between the 1960s and 1970s suggests that over this period the educational system has become increasingly selective. In other words, the data from the present study suggests that there has been a significant reversal of the trend towards greater equality of opportunity in the educational system which Peil believed that she had discovered.

This reduction in the proportion of students who have been inter-generationally mobile is associated with a decline in the proportion of those who have been intra-grenerationally mobile as can be seen from Table 23. In particular, the proportion of students coming to university after working for some time has fallen from two thirds twenty years ago to less than one third at the time of the present study. In the same period, on the other hand, the proportion of students who had attended sixth form rose from between 60 per cent and 70 per cent to over 80 per cent.[25] As explained previously, such a reduction in the proportion of students qualifying for university through private studies is likely to reduce not only intra-generational mobility for the individuals concerned, but also the potential for inter-generational mobility in the society as a whole, for most

TABLE 23

**Proportion of Legon Students who had been
Employed before Entering University**

Academic Year	%
1953	[b] 63.0
1957	[d] 63.5
1960	[d] 52.9
1963	[d] 53.9
1973	[c] 30.4

a.   Jahoda 1954, p.357.
b.   Peil 1965, p.26.
c.   Data from the present study.

students coming to university by the "backdoor" are drawn from homes of lower than average socio-economic status.

In more general terms, the decline in the proportion of students from lower status homes may be attributed to various structural features of Ghanaian society. As in other developing societies, the rate of upward mobility is severely constrained by the small size of the elite, which constitutes only between 1 per cent and 5 per cent of the total population, depending on the classification used.[26] Most of the upward mobility which does occur is what sociologists call "forced mobility", for it depends on the relatively rapid expansion of this small elite as socio-economic development proceeds.[27] In this type of mobility, elite parents are usually able to manipulate the basic inequity of the educational system so as to secure this socio-economic position for their children — i.e. there is relatively little downward mobility between generations — while a substantial number of the children of non-elite children are able to move up to fill the new opennings made available by the expansion of the elite.[28] But of course this mobility, though it may be seen substantial from the point of view of the tiny elite, is actually quite minimal when viewed relative to the vast mass of the population which occupies non-elite positions; and in addition, as Fox and Miller imply, such mobility is the result of rather special circumstances and does not necessarily indicate any intrinsic openness in the social structure (Fox and Miller 1967: 575).

The real test for such mobility comes when the rate of expansion of the elite slows down, as it tends to do for purely mathematical reasons, as well as because of the generally sluggish nature of the economy in most neo-colonial states.[29] In this case, either some children of elite parents will have to be downwardly mobile to allow lower status children to move up and replace them through "exchange mobility", or else a decreasing proportion of the elite will be drawn from non-elite homes. From the data presented above, it would seem that the latter pattern most closely resembles the situation in contemporary Ghana, presumably because the children of better-off parents are able to take full advantage of the inequalities inherent in the educational system. As a result, they will probably increasingly monopolize the higher status positions within society. Children from poorer homes, on the other hand, are likely to find it more and more difficult to rise to the highest levels in the socio-economic hierarchy unless radical changes which are instituted in the educational system. But, for reasons which will be explained in the final section of this paper, such radical changes are unlikely to be brought about within the framework set by the present socio-political structure of Ghanaian society.

Conclusions and Discussion

Although, as pointed out in the introduction, the data presented in this paper are not entirely satisfactory, they do suggest certain conclusions about the pattern of social mobility in contemporary Ghana. In the first place, although they give some support to the conclusions of Clignet and Foster that a relatively high proportion of students in institutions of higher education in West Africa are drawn from lower status homes, they also show considerable inequality between children from different types of backgrounds in their chances of acquiring the level of education which would qualify them for the most highly-rewarded positions in society. In fact, it would appear that most of the children of elite parents are able to secure elite, or at least, sub-elite positions for themselves. However, this is true of only a very small proportion of the much larger number of young people with lower status backgrounds and in this way, privilege (or underprivilege) is perpetuated from one generation to the next. In addition, it was suggested that the upward mobility which is occurring in present-day Ghana does not indicate the existence of a genuinely open type of social structure but mainly results from rather special circumstances, particularly the expansion of elite positions as economic development proceeds. The proportion of such opportunities is likely to experience a relative decline in the future, however, as the rate of economic development shows up and indeed, the effect of this may already be manifest in the data presented in this paper which suggest a reduction in the proportion of the elite being drawn from lower status homes. The main conclusions of this paper, then, are that the stratification system of Ghana is essentially characterized by inequality rather than equality of opportunity, and that, though this may be partially disguised at present, it is likely to become increasingly evident with the passage of time.

It would seem possible that educational reform may do something to remedy this situation by stimulating an increase in the rate of upward social mobility. Indeed, it seems probable that Nkrumah's Accelerated Development Plan for Education, 1951, had such an effect, and that this may explain the "broadening base" of Legon students as encountered by Peil in the late fifties and early sixties.[30] More recent changes in the educational system, however — such as the spread of "international" preparatory schools, the shortened period spent in elementary school, the rising cost of secondary education (particularly when taken together with the general increase in the cost of living), the rising level of qualifications required for entry into university and the tendency to recruit an increasing proportion of undergraduates directly from sixth form — have usually been regressive insofar as they are likely to reduce opportunities for upward social mobility through higher education. This would also be true, other things being equal, of the kind of policy discussed in this paper which would systematically discriminate against students in "non-priority" areas, for example, by artificially limiting their numbers, forcing them to pay their own tuition fees and find their own accommodation and by refusing study-leave with pay to teachers who wished to read such subjects at university.

For a number of reasons, the present author is sceptical about the possibility of educational reform having any significant positive effects on rates of social mobility, at least in the short run. Firstly, from a purely practical point of view, it will be much more difficult for present-day educational planners to bring about an effect equivalent to that of Nkrumah's reforms precisely because these earlier reforms have already been carried out and the educational system today is, therefore, so much larger and more complex than that which confronted Nkrumah during the latter days of colonial rule. Secondly, from a political point of view, it would seem that the kind of radical reforms required are unlikely at this stage for they would be in contradiction with the class structure of existing society; and in particular, they would be detrimental to the interests of members of the politically articulate and influential upper classes who are concerned to perpetuate the privileged position which they and their children enjoy under the present system.[31] More mild measures of reform, which would be politically acceptable to the ruling classes, are likely to be relatively ineffectual. This would be so because the educational system remains enclosed within a social structure which is essentially based on inequality, and, as can be seen from the histories of similar reforms in other stratified societies, members of the already privileged strata are usually able to neutralize their redistributive provisions, or even turn them to their own advantage.[32] It is, therefore, apparent that educational reform cannot be viewed in isolation from conditions in the rest of society: in fact, it is likely to have relatively little effect unless it is accompanied by an overall restructuring of society as whole. Pressures for such radical changes involving not only the educational system but also the whole society are obviously unlikely to come from members of the presently privileged elite who benefit under the existing system, but rather from members of the under-privileged strata who, according to the results of this paper, are being increasingly excluded from the opportunity of sharing these benefits. Up to now, however, the latter have tended to form a politically mute section of the population.

This brings us back finally to the relationship mentioned in the first section of this paper between social mobility and political stability. It was argued there that a widespread beliefs in the existence of opportunities for upward social mobility are among the factors discouraging the emergency of class consciousness among members of the lower strata in contemporary African societies and that this contributes to the political stability of these societies. But if opportunities for those of lower status origins to enter the elite have declined relative to those from more privileged backgrounds, as suggested in this paper, what will be the consequences for political stability?

It is quite possible that it will make very little difference. Some opportunities for upward mobility will of course remain — indeed they may even increase in absolute, though not in relative terms — and members of the under-privileged strata may either not realize that their position has deteriorated relative to those from better-off strata, or (with the gambling inclination of the poor everywhere) they may still consider that they will be among·the lucky ones who will benefit from those opportunities which remain.[33] In this case they may continue to be committed to improving their own position through individual upward mobility rather than through class action. Even when they have discounted the possibility of improving their own position through individual upward mobility, however, members of the under-privileged strata may still remain essentially unrevolutionary. They may accept the system of inequality as legitimate — for example resulting from the will of God — or the method of social selection as basically fair and in either case, they are likely to come to some kind of accommodation with the system based on a low level of personal aspirations.[34] The most likely outcome of the situation probably lies among the above possibilities, and all of them appear to favour the socio-political status quo.

If, however, as a result of the relative deterioration in their chances of entering the elite, members of the lower socio-economic strata were to become disillusioned with the present system of social stratification, this might have revolutionary political consequences. It might contribute to the development of class consciousness, hitherto masked by beliefs in the possibility of social mobility, among members of the less privileged strata and hence, to their emergency as a "class-for-itself". This class might then be responsible for the simultaneous transformation of both the educational system and the society which contains it; and in fact, as suggested above, this may be the only sure road to educational reform.

NOTES

1.   The research on which this paper is based was financed by a generous grant from the United Nations Development Programme, from their Special Fund for Population Activities. A first draft of the paper was presented to the Population and Education Study Seminar at the University of Cape Coast in 1976, and my thanks are due to the seminar organizer, Mr. Willie Henderson, other participants and to Dr. Margaret Peil of the Centre of West African Studies, University of Birmingham, for their helpful comments, many of which have been incorporated in the present paper.

I would also like to thank the Registrar and his staff at the University of Ghana for their kind cooperation in allowing the necessary data to be collected from their records; and my graduate research assistant, Mr. Sampson Asare, who was responsible for collecting and coding most of the data.

2. See, for example, the work of Jahoda (1954/5), Foster (1963 and 1965), Clignet and Foster (1966), Peil (1965), and Hurd and Johnson (1967).

3. For the classical formulation of the functional theory of social stratification, see Davies and Moore (1945).

4. This distinction arises at several points in Marx's work, but is perhaps best known from his *The Eighteenth Brunaire of Louis Napoleon.*

5. This point of view has been particularly associated with the work of Peter Lloyd. See, for example, Lloyd (1966, pp. 335–9; 1973, pp. 122–4; and 1974).

6. See, for example, Jahoda, *op. cit.;* Peil, *op. cit.;* and Hurd and Johnson, *op. cit.*

7. For example, the main index of a student's socio-economic background to be derived from his file must be based on the occupation of his "next-of-kin", though fathers' occupations normally provide the base-line in such inter-generational studies of social mobility and, in addition, the occupation of next-of-kin may be given in a very vague or generalized form — such as civil servant, businessman, farmer, soldier, or pensioner — which makes it difficult to locate this person at any specific level in the socio-economic hierarchy.

8. Of course, it might be argued that collection of data by such means is unethical, for confidential information about the students is used in the study without their permission having first been obtained.

9. Information could not be obtained on about 76 students, of whom 35 were in the Faculty of Science and 29 in the Faculty of Medicine. In the case of the Science students, this was probably because of the deliberate exclusion of fourth year honours students; while in the case of medical students, it was possibly because their files had been removed to the Medical School, which is situated at some distance from the main university campus.

10. Other possible indices of students' geographical origins are their hometowns, or their places of current residence. Information on these was collected, but their use would not have changed the main conclusion of this paper, though the former would have suggested that students came from rather smaller settlements and the latter from rather larger settlements than the present results indicate. They were not used, however, mainly because they do not necessarily indicate the kind of environment in which the students were brought up, which is the main point of interest here; and,

in addition, the data on home-towns are even less comparable with census figures than those on places of birth, for the census gives the distribution of the population by place of residence and not by home-town. Perhaps the best indices would be in the form of "place of longest residence during the first ten years of life", as used by Hurd and Johnson (*op. cit.,* p.63); but of course such information is not available on the student files.

11. Even as long ago as 1948, Fortes could write of the Ashanti Region: "The demand for schools is sweeping the country. It is the outstanding instance of a matter on which almost full unanimity is found in every community, for which the people everywhere are prepared to make substantial economic sacrifices, and to promote and for which they are ready to drop factional differences". (Fortes 1948: 32)

12. As explained in note "7", occupation of the next-of-kin of students was used because it was what was available in their files. It should be noted, however, that this may be just as good an indication as their parents' occupation of the financial resources available within the extended family which can be used to promote their educational careers. The actual distribution of their next-of-kin was as follows: fathers, 63 per cent; mothers, 11 per cent, brothers, 10 per cent; uncles, 10 per cent; others and "don't knows", 6 per cent. These kinship terms, of course, should be understood in a classificatory sense rather than in a purely biological sense.

To understand the occupational classification which was used, some examples may be noted, as follows:–

Professionals:	doctors, lawyers, priests, army officers, university lecturers, administrative grade civil servants, managers, etc.
Lower professionals:	teachers, nurses, technicians, librarians, surveyors, executive grade civil servants, etc.
Clerical:	clerks, ungraded civil servants, other ranks of army and police, supervisors, foremen, etc.
Higher commercial:	transport owners, wholesale merchants, cocoa buyers, contractors, etc.
Lower commercial:	petty traders, foodsellers, fishmongers
Skilled manual:	carpenters, fitters tailors, etc. (both in employment and self-employed)
Semi-skilled:	drivers, cooks, messengers, etc.
Unskilled:	labourers, watchmen, etc.
Agricultural:	farmers, farm labourers, fishermen, etc.
Excluded from analysis:	non-workers, such as housewives, students, and pensioners who could not be otherwise classified.

13. A relatively high proportion of students appear to have their next-of-kin in lower commercial occupations, but it should be realized that this is rather

misleading. For in most cases, this refers to their mothers. Many of these women may have actually been quite wealthy, though they have generally been coded as "petty traders" because of lack of adequate evidence — in fact, distinguishing between those in higher commercial and lower commercial occupations was one of the most difficult coding decisions which had to be made. In addition, many of these students who named their mothers as their next-of-kin may have been able to call on other better-off male relatives for financial assistance with their education. It should also be noted that as many lower commercial next-of-kin are females, it is not really legitimate to compare them with the proportion of lower commercial workers in the *male* labour force, as is done in Table 16. Instead, they should be compared with the much larger proportion of such workers in the *female* labour force, which would give a very different impression.

14.   The importance of "international" preparatory schools in this context is emphasized by Addae-Mensah, Djangmah and Agbenyegah (N.D.).

15.   On the generally lower level of aspiration of female students in West Africa, see Foster, *op. cit.* (1965), ch. 8; and Clignet and Foster, *op. cit.,* ch. 6.

16.   The educational backwardness of female students may also possibly be attributed to the lack of adequate educational facilities for them, despite constant lip service being paid to the need to promote female education.

17.   It may be noted that the proportion of students of Volta Region origin is even higher than these figures suggests, for many with their home-towns in the Volta Region were born outside it, presumably as a result of their parents having migrated to find work.

18.   Thus, Peil found that only 1.6 per cent of her sample had been born in the Northern and Upper Regions as compared with 5.6 per cent among students included in the present survey (See Peil, *op. cit.,* p.24).

19.   Actually, Foster found that *within* the secondary system, the children of elite parents were disproportionately represented at only the two highest status schools, namely Achimota and Mfanstipim; but it seems quite likely that since his study, social selectivity may have become a more pervasive feature of the educational system at this level. See Foster, *op. cit.,* (1965), pp. 352–4.

20.   For an outline of the pattern of educational and occupational aspirations among secondary school students in West Africa, see Foster, *Ibid.,* ch, 8; and Clignet and Foster, *op. cit.,* ch. 6.

21.   For an outline of this policy, see *The Ghanaian Times,* September 15, 1976, p.1.

22. It may also be noted that students from Legon tend to come from more privileged socio-economic backgrounds than those at the less prestigious University of Cape Coast. See Sinclair (1975, pp. 10–13; and 1976, pp. 93, 109–10).

23. As Miller points out, "benchmarks" to allow assessment of rates of social mobility may also be provided by comparative studies (Miller, 1960, p.1).

24. This increasing social selectivity in the student population may also be noted among the students in the 1973/4 sample. Thus among third year students at Legon during the 1973/4 academic session, 35 per cent came from professional, administrative, managerial and executive homes, and 35 per cent were also from agricultural and manual homes, while among the new entrants (i.e. first year students), 42 per cent were from the former type of homes, and only 32 per cent from the latter.

25. For the earlier figures, see Jahoda, *op. cit.,* p.357; and Peil, *op. cit.,* pp. 25–6.

26. For a comparison, it may be noted that in the United States, over 40 per cent of workers are in white-collar occupations, while only about 5 per cent are employed in agriculture and related activities.

27. For the use of the term "forced mobility", see Yasuda (1964, p.16). He, however, contrasts it with what he calls "pure mobility", while in the present study the term "exchange mobility" has been preferred for this other type.

28. Bibby and Peil have recently challenged the general belief that there is little downward mobility in Ghanaian society, but as yet, their evidence seems too narrowly-based to be acceptable (Bibby and Peil, 1974, pp. 412–7).

29. An indication of this relatively slow expansion of the elite may be found by comparing the occupational distribution of employed males in 1970 with that of 1960, as shown in Table 22.

30. In this case we could discriminate between Bibby's criticisms of Peil's results and conclude that the effect which she detected was "transitory" but not necessarily "illusory". See Bibby (1973, p.371).

31. It is not being suggested that educational planners and policy makers necessarily, deliberately discriminate against lower status children — indeed, they may even hope that their reforms will help such children — but insofar as they are working within limited financial resources, they may be unwilling to consider plans which would handicap their own children and then their policies will probably have such a regressive effect. In addition, if the educational system is to be judged mainly in terms of the efficiency of its contribution to the bourgeois ideal of national economic development, as

seems to be the present policy, then this will involve taking pragmatic academic decisions about the selection and training of university students which may come into conflict with the principle of egalitarianism. Such a conflict has been very apparent in recent years in the Chinese educational system.

32. For evidence about this in the British situation, see Abel-Smith (1958) and Westergaard (1964).

33. Gambling itself may act as a "safety valve" for the system, for it encourages even those who have least possibility of achieving social mobility by conventional means to believe that they can improve their position in society; and they need no other qualification for this than luck. This presumably explains the popularity of "Lotto" in Ghana. For an analysis of this stabilizing function of gambling, see Parkin (1972, pp. 76–8).

34. There is some evidence from Peil's study of factory workers in Ghana that they are coming to such an accommodation. See Peil (192, pp. 110–15).

REFERENCES

Abel-Smith, B. (1958). "Whose Welfare State?", in N. MacKenzie (ed). *Conviction.* London: MacGibbon and Kee.

Achebe, G. (1960). *No Longer at Ease.* London: Heinemann.

Addae-Mensah, I., Djangmah, J. S., and Agbenyegah, C. O. (n.d.), *Family Background and Educational Opportunities in Ghana.* University of Cape Coast: unpublished manuscript.

Bibby, J., (1973). "The Social Base of Ghanaian Education: is it still broadening?" *British Journal of Sociology,* Vol. 24, No. 3, pp. 365–74.

Bibby, J., and Peil, M. (1974). "Secondary Education in Ghana: Private Enterprise and Social Selection", *Sociology of Education,* Vol. 47, No. 3, pp. 399–418.

Clignet, R. and Foster, P. (1966). *The Fortunate Few: A Study of Secondary School Students in the Ivory Coast.* Chicago: North Western University Press.

Davies, K. and Moore, W. E. (1945). "Some Principles of Stratification", *American Sociological Review,* Vol. 10, No. 2, pp. 242–9.

Fortes, M. (1948). "The Ashanti Social Survey: A Preliminary Report". *Rhodes-Livingstone Journal,* No. 6, pp. 1–36.

Foster, P. (1963). "Secondary Schooling and Social Mobility in a West African Nation", *Sociology of Education,* Vol. 37, No. 2, pp. 150–71.

Foster, P. (1965). *Education and Social Change in Ghana.* London: Routledge and Kegan Paul.

Foster, P. (1968). "Comments on Hurd and Johnson", *Sociology of Education,* Vol. 41, No. 1, pp. 111–5.

Fox, T. and Miller, S. M. (1967). "Intra-Country Variations: Occupational Stratification and Mobility", in R. Bendix and S. M. Lipset (eds.), *Class, Status and Power: A Comparative Perspective.* London: Routledge and Kegan Paul.

Hurd, G. E. and Johnson, T. J. (1967). "Education and Social Mobility in Ghana", *Sociology of Education,* Vol. 40, No. 1, pp. 55–79.

Jahoda, G. (1954–5). "The Social Background of a West African Student Population", *British Journal of Sociology,* Part I, Vol. 5, No. 4, pp. 355–65, and Part II, Vol. 6, No. 1, pp. 71–9.

Little, A. and Westergaard, J. (1964). "The Trend of Class Differentials in Educational Opportunity in England and Wales", *British Journal of Sociology,* Vol. 15, No. 4, pp. 301–16.

Lloyd, P. C. (1966). "Class Consciousness among the Yoruba", in P. C. Lloyd (ed.), *The New Elites of Tropical Africa.* London: Oxford University Press for the International African Institute.

Lloyd, P. C. (1973). *Classes, Crises and Coups: Themes in the Sociology of Developing Societies.* London: Paladin.

Lloyd, P. C. (1974). *Power and Independence: Urban Africans' Perception of Social Inequality.* London: Routledge and Kegan Paul.

Miller, S. M. (1960). "Comparative Social Mobility: A Trend Report", *Current Sociology,* Vol. 9, No. 1, pp. 1–89.

Ofuatey-Kodjoe, W. (1974). "Education and Social change in Africa: Some Proposals", *Ghana Journal of Sociology,* Vol. 8, No. 2, pp. 5–15.

Parkin, F. (1972). *Class Inequality and Political Order: Social Stratification in Capitalist and Communist Societies.* London: Paladin.

Peil, M. (1965). "Ghanaian University Students: The Broadening Base". *British Journal of Sociology,* Vol. 16, No. 1, pp. 19–28.

Peil M. (1972). *The Ghanaian Factory Worker: Industrial Man in Africa.* Cambridge: Cambridge University Press.

Plotnicov, L. (1970). "The Modern African Elite in Jos, Nigeria", in A Tuden and L. Plotnicov (eds.), *Social Stratification in Africa.* London: Collier-MacMillan Ltd.

Sinclair, J. S. (1975). "Some Characteristics of the Student Population in the University of Cape Coast", *The Oguaa Educator,* Vol. 5, No. 2, pp. 4–15.

Sinclair, J. S. (1976). "Social Mobility and the Characteristics of Students at the University of Ghana (Legon)", in W. Henderson (ed.), *Population and Education Study Seminar Report.* University of Cape Coast: Centre for Educational Planning and Research.

Yasuda, S. (1964). "A Methodological Inquiry into Social Mobility", *American Sociological Review,* Vol. 29, No. 1, pp. 16–23.

3.   **Mobilization of Rural Resources for Community Development***

K. M. Ganu

We saw in Chapter 5 that rural people are essentially dependent on informal sources of credit to finance agricultural production. This, nevertheless, has resulted in increased output and incomes of the people. Plausibly, this would lead to improved standard of living and reduction of rural poverty which are the main objectives of rural development. In this chapter, we examine the savings behaviour of rural people, the extent to which improved standard of living is related to community development and the development priorities of rural people.

6.1   Mobilization of Savings for Rural Development

The importance of rural savings as a source of locally generated loanable funds had often been forgotten by scholars and policy-makers. Thus, all rural finance projects in developing countries have stressed low interest loans for agriculture to the total neglect of savings mobilization in the rural areas (Adams and Vogel 1986: 484). This neglect of rural savings meant that continuous flow of funds to official rural credit schemes would be hamstringed. In this study, therefore, we examined the savings behaviour of rural people and the role of rural financial institutions in mobilizing savings for development.

6.1.1.   *Savings Behaviour of Rural People*
In our examination of the savings behaviour of rural people, we saw that the majority (205) or 82.7 per cent of the entire sample saves some money from their income stream, while 17.3 per cent do not save at all. The distribution by locality indicates that 84.8 per cent of the respondents at Vodza, 73.9 per cent at Agbledomi-Dzita, 76.2 per cent at Fiahor and 88.4 per cent at Abor saved. Although there is no significant difference in the proportion of the respondents who saved in the four localities, it is noted that Agbledomi-Dzita which is the least developed of the four localities has the lowest proportion of savers.

We also obtained data on the various avenues used by respondents for saving. The study reveals that 22.4 per cent of savers used rotating credit societies (*susu*), 2 per cent saved with cooperative credit unions, 39.5 per cent with the bank, 35.6 per cent in their homes and one person (0.5 per cent) saved with the grandmother. The bank is the most important avenue

* Culled from Ganu, K. M. (1991) *op. cit.,* Chapter 6. Published by kind permission of the author and the Faculty of Social Sciences, University of Cape Coast, Cape Coast.

for savings in the four localities, but we realized, however, that this situation was due to the over 50 per cent of respondent at Abor who saved with the bank. Table 24 shows the distribution of the sample among saving avenues by locality.

TABLE 24[1]

Savings Avenues Used by Respondents by Locality
(In Percentages)

Saving Avenues	Locality			
	Vodza (N = 39)	Agbledomi-Dzita (N = 51)	Fiahor (N = 16)	Abor (N = 99)
Rotating Credit Societies	10.2	7.8	18.8	35.4
Cooperative Credit Union	0.0	0.0	0.0	4.0
Bank	35.9	27.5	18.8	50.5
Self (Home)	51.3	64.7	62.5	10.1
Other (With Grandmother)	2.6	0.0	0.0	0.0
Total	100.0	100.0	100.1[2]	100.0

Note: [1] Tables 24–35 refer to Tables 6.1–6.12 in the original thesis.
[2] Total greater than 100 due to rounding up.

As expected, majority of respondents at Abor (54.4 per cent), channelled their savings through the formal sector (Cooperative Credit Union and Bank). Rotation Credit Societies were also very important there. On the other hand, the majority of respondents at Vodza (51.3 per cent), Agbledomi-Dzita (64.7 per cent) and Fiahor (62.5 per cent) saved in their homes (self). In the economics literature, any savings outside the banking system is tantamount to hoarding (Kurihara 1970: 107). It is believed that such hoarded money could not be channelled into loanable funds by the banking system if they were not saved at the banks. In the rural communities, however, such "hoarded" funds provide quick and on the spot credit to the majority of borrowers who depend on the informal sector. To bring this large proportion of savers into the banking system will require, not only an aggressive savings mobilization strategy by rural financial institutions, but also offering positive real rates of interest on savings to make "hoarding" unattractive.

6.1.2   *Benefits from Savings*

For the community as a whole, increased savings means greater availability of loanable funds in both the formal and informal sectors of credit. This is important for the health of the rural economy. For, as seen in Chapter 5, access to credit leads to increased output and incomes and consequently, improved standard of living of rural people. At the individual level, respondents were asked to mention up to two benefits that could be derived from savings. Table 25 presents the frequency distribution of the responses.

TABLE 25

Distribution of Benefits Respondents could Derive from Savings (In Percentages)

Benefits	First Response (N = 221)[1]	Second Response (N = 71)
No Benefits	2.7	0.0
Interest paid on the deposit	18.1	1.4
Provides for emergency	67.9	22.5
Easier access to bank credit	9.2	73.2
Others[2]	1.8	2.8

Notes: 1. Includes 16 who do not save but answered the question.
         2. Includes: security, and to buy future needs.

We noted from Table 25 that 221 respondents named only one benefit while 71 of them mentioned two. In the first instance we found that 67.9 per cent, saved because saving provides ready funds for any emergency expenditure one has to make. At the second instance, 73.2 per cent of the respondents thought that it gives them easier access to bank credit. About 18 per cent of the respondents thought that savers benefited from the interest paid on their deposits. In this respect, positive real interest rates offered by the banks would have the potential for attracting more savers to the banking system.

Finally, the 43 respondents who did not save were asked to give reasons for not doing so. The survey indicates that 87.8 per cent did not have enough money to save, 7.3 per cent were not actively working and 2.8 per cent said they had too many dependants. Two people failed to respond.

6.1.3   The Role of Rural Financial Institutions

One argument for savings mobilization by rural credit institutions is that their very viability and effectiveness in rural credit delivery depend on the continual flow of internally generated funds for lending (Adams and Vogel 1986: 486). In this study, therefore, we also examined the extent of savings mobilization by the financial institutions serving the Keta district — based on the returns from four bank branches.

First, we obtained data on the mobilization of customers by the four banks. Table 26 presents the number of customers in each bank by type of account as at 31st December, 1988 and 31st December, 1989.

TABLE 26

Distribution of Bank Customers by Types of Account
as at 31/12/1988 and 31/12/1989

Name of Bank	Year of Establishment	Number of Customers			
		1988		1989	
		Current	Saving	Current	Saving
G.C.B., Keta	1962	908	6,295	674	6,334
G.C.B., Abor	1977	534	4,742	548	4,949
C.B., Anloga	1977	1,077	1,969	956	1,785
V.P.R.B., Dzelukope[1]	1979	7,129	10,276	7,529	11,791
Total		9,648	23,273	9,707	24,859

Note: [1] Includes customers at the two agencies at Anloga and Anyanui.

As should be expected, all the banks have more savings account customers than current account holders. In all, there were 32,921 accounts in the 4 banks as at 31st December, 1988 and 34,566 accounts by 31st December, 1989 — a mere 5 per cent increase. Contrary to expectation, the youngest of the four banks, Volta Premier Rural Bank (VPRB), had mobilized more customers than all the other banks. Indeed, the bank had 73.9 per cent of all current account customers in 1988 and 77.6 per cent in 1989. It also had 44.2 per cent and 47.4 per cent of savings account customers in 1988 and 1989 respectively. This, however, is not surprising because as a rural bank and a unit bank at that, its loanable funds must be locally generated. Secondly, the less stringent conditions offered by the bank also make the rural bank a better alternative for rural people. Finally, the bank was able to mobilize more customers through its agency operations and offer of commodity loans (see section 6.2.4). We also noted from Table 26 that the Ghana Cooperative Bank (C.B.) at Anloga is the least in the mobilization of customers.

We then obtained data on total deposits and withdrawals from the four banks for the period, January 1988 to June 1990. Table 27 shows that although the VPRB topped the table in mobilizing more customers (Table 26), it was pushed to third position in actual amount of money deposited by customers. As expected, the administrative and commercial functions of Keta, the district capital, explain the dominant position of Ghana Commercial Bank (G.C.B.), Keta in deposit mobilization. Indeed the bank had higher average deposit per customer than all the other three banks. Calculations from 1989 figures in Table 26 and 27 for instance, reveal that the bank had an average deposit of ¢212,448.09 per customer. The GCB at Abor had ¢185,875.48 per customer, CB at Anloga had ¢49,565.57 and VPRB at Dzelukope had ¢33,954.45. It can, therefore, be inferred that the rural bank is more appealing to a large number of small savers than the commercial banks.

TABLE 27

Distribution of Deposits in the Four Banks Studied

Name of Banks	Total Deposits in Cedis		
	1988	1989	1990
G.C.B., Keta	1,153,889,456	1,488,836,220	826,470,286
G.C.B., Abor	814,513,962	1,021,757,560	400,133,408
C.B., Anloga	140,764,923	135,859,23	—
V.P.R.B., Dzelukope	246,000,000	656,000,000	422,000,000
Total	2,355,168,341	3,302,453,017	1,648,603,614

In order to ascertain the amount of internally generated loanable funds of the banks, we matched total deposits against total withdrawals. For the four banks, we had withdrawals totalling ¢2,348,716,004 in 1988 — leaving an excess of ¢6,452,337 of deposits over withdrawals. In 1989 withdrawals amounted to ¢2,987,724,344 leaving an excess of ¢314,728,673, and up to 30th June, 1990 withdrawals from the three banks were ¢1,372,871,457 with an excess of ¢276,732,157. Thus, in all, there was always an excess of deposits over withdrawals which could be channelled into loans. Table 28 presents how the four banks fared in generating loanable funds internally in 1989.

TABLE 28

Generation of Loanable Funds by the Four Banks in 1989

Name of Bank 1	Deposits 2 (¢)	Withdrawals 3 (¢)	Loanable Fund 4 (2–3) (¢)	Amount of Loans Granted 5 (¢)
G.C.B., Keta	1,488,386,220	1,423,437,767	63,398,454	N/R
G.C.B., Abor	1,021,757,560	892,939,134	128,818,426	N/R
C.B., Anloga	135,859,237	122,347,443	13,511,794	10,322,000
V.P.R.B., Dzelukope	656,000,000	547,000,000	109,000,000	55,000,000

Note: NR = Non-response.

Unfortunately, the two GCB branches at Keta and Abor, failed to provide data on loans granted. Loans extended by CB, Anloga and VPRB, Dzelukope, were however, less than the internally generated loanable funds. While that of the Ghana Cooperative Bank was quite precarious, the VPRB loaned out approximately 50.5 per cent of its internally generated loanable fund. Since we have lending records for only two banks, we can only conjecture that given the level of deposits against withdrawals the credit institutions in the district are capable of mobilizing enough resources locally to ensure their viability.

Finally, we have observed that most rural people are socially distanced from rural financial institutions due to illiteracy and ignorance (section 5.5.4, Chapter 5). In this connection, we asked the credit institutions what they were doing to educate rural people on banking. Four main measures were listed by the banks. First, they organized talks and open fora at the community level to educate rural people on banking. Secondly, they encourage non-account holders, through their own customers, to open accounts. Again, bank officials attend meetings of Cooperative Societies and offer advice to members about facilities opened to them at the banks. Finally, education is carried on through the Information Services Department (there was no indication in the response from GCB, Abor, as to how the Information Services Department was used). These activities were aimed at enhancing the deposit mobilization capacity of the banks which is considered essential for their self-sufficiency.

6.1.4 Special Position of Rural Banks

The important role being played by rural banks in the rural credit system in Ghana has been stressed by many scholars and policy-makers. In an interview with *West Africa,* Professor Patrick Twumasi observed that:

> Rural banking is a loudable concept for financing rural development. But the fact that [in Ghana], it was imposed from above without evolving from within the communities, for example, through the *susu* system makes the banks lord it over them [rural dwellers] (*West Africa,* 28th March to 1st April, 1990).

In view of the above, Professor Twumasi thinks that rural dwellers do not appreciate the value of rural banks in their economic ventures. However, in our examination of the extent of rural people's awareness of rural banks and their willingness to contribute capital towards the establishment of a rural bank in their communities, we found that 93.5 per cent of the respondents were aware of the existence of rural banks and this confirmed Brown's findings (Brown 1984: 51). The respondents were also asked to mention as many benefits as they thought rural people could derive from rural banks. Table 29 presents the multiple responses of the sample. The distribution shows that 98 per cent felt that rural people would benefit from rural banks. Secondly, the provision of facility for savings was the modal benefit rural people thought they would derive from rural banks. This was followed by: "provision of commodity loans (48 per cent); provision of loans for agriculture (38.2 per cent) and longer payment period for loans (33.3 per cent)". Evidently, savings mobilization is perceived by the respondents as the most important single benefit which rural banks provide for the people (see section 6.1.3).

Finally, we asked respondents whether they would support the establishment of a rural bank in their community through equity participation. To this, 78.6 per cent of the respondents said they would buy shares. Those who would not buy shares in rural banks (53 respondents) were asked why they would not do so. The majority (71.2 per cent) responded that they did not have enough money to do so while 13.5 per cent said they did not understand how it worked; 7.7 per cent said they were not interested; 1.9 per cent (1 person) said he was too old to buy shares and 5.8 per cent mentioned "other" reasons such as: "prefer to save, only rich people would use the money, the banks may be sited elsewhere and not yet earning income". Plausibly, with increased incomes and education, rural people would willingly support rural financial intermediaries to mobilize enough resources from their catchment areas, both as equity capital and as deposits to make them more effective and self-supporting.

TABLE 29

**Distribution of Multiple Responses of Benefits Rural
People Could Derive from Rural Banks
(In Percentages)**

Benefit (N = 246)[1]	Response to Item		
	Yes	No	Total
No benefit	2.0	98.0	100.0
Provide facility for saving	48.8	51.2	100.0
Provide finance for agriculture	38.2	61.8	100.0
Help rural development	32.1	67.9	100.0
Provide commodity loans	48.0	52.0	100.0
Give longer payment period for loans	33.3	66.7	100.0
Demand collaterals rural people can offer	1.2	98.8	100.0
Other[2]	6.9	93.1	100.0

Notes: 1. Non-response = 2
2. Includes: assist traders, educate rural people on banking and don't
know.

6.2   Community Development

Community development is aimed at motivating the rural communities to
participate actively in community affairs through self-help projects and adult
education (Ewusi 1978: 77). It involves the provision of basic socio-economic
infrastructure such as schools and colleges, hospitals, motorable roads,
good drinking water, public toilet, electricity and community centres, among
others, in the rural communities. These facilities are expected to bridge the
development gap between the rural and urban areas and reduce rural
deprivation and poverty.

6.2.1   *Community Needs*
We have noted, in section 3.5 of Chapter 3, the facilities available at
present in the four localities. We saw that with the exception of Abor, the
other three localities were grossly deficient in community facilities such
as good drinking water, public latrines, motorable roads and health cen-

tres. Even at Abor, the existing ones were quite inadequate. We, therefore, asked respondents to list the socio-economic facilities they needed in their communities. For Vodza, the following needs were recorded: public toilet/ latrine, pipe-borne water, good roads, electricity supply, health centre, Junior Secondary School, a bank, community centre and football park. At Agbledomi-Dzita, the following needs were listed: public toilet/latrine, pipe-borne water, good roads, electricity, health centre, second-cycle school, agricultural inputs supply depot, community centre, a market and a post office. At Fiahor, the following needs were also listed: public well water or pipe-borne water, good roads, electricity, junior secondary school, a police station, a bank, transport services, community centre, a market and a post office. Finally, for Abor, the following needs were listed: public toilet, pipe-borne water, electricity, tractor hiring service, community centre and a market.

Surprisingly, 17 per cent of the respondents at Abor listed agriculture extension office even though Abor already had one. This could be explained in terms of lack of awareness of the existence of the extension service. We also noted that the need for pipe-borne water, electricity supply and community centre was common to all the four localities. Only Fiahor did not indicate their need for a public toilet, most probably because they had one.

6.2.2   Who Should Provide Community Facilities?

We saw in section 3.5, Chapter 3, that with the exception of the health centre serving Fiahor and the Information Services Department, the Post Office, the Ghana Commercial Bank — all at Abor, which were provided by the government, all the social amenities existing in the four localities were either provided by the people themselves through self-help or by churches.

In this regard, respondents were asked to indicate who should provide the facilities that the community needed. The multiple responses for 245 respondents show that 78.6 per cent named the central government, 24.6 per cent named the district assembly and 60.1 per cent mentioned the community. Indeed, most people (including rural dwellers) look up to the central government as the most important agent that can bring about rural development. In a study of students at the University of Ghana, Legon, Brown (1981/82: 27–60) observes that 91 per cent of the students also put the onus on the central government for the provision of social amenities in the rural areas. Thus, if we view rural people as producing the bulk of the nation's wealth, then they deserve nothing but a fair share of this wealth. This then explains the majority view that the central government should provide social amenities in the rural areas. Secondly, the over 60 per cent of the respondents who mentioned "the community" provides sufficient evidence that rural people are prepared to participate actively in the development of their own communities (*see* also Agyeman 1987: 96–98). Finally, the district assembly was the least important — indicating that the role of the assemblies in rural development is not yet fully appreciated by small communities.

6.2.3   Contribution of Resources towards Community Development

If rural credit leads to improved standard of living of rural people, one would expect that the people would be willing to provide resources such as communal labour and funds for their development projects. When respondents were asked whether they would contribute more towards the development of their community if their incomes increased the entire sample indicated that they would do so. As to the nature of the contribution they would make the multiple responses were: "contribution of free labour, 91.9 per cent; contribution of cash (money), 27.9 per cent; and free participation in community fishing (*eduɔ dada*), 0.8 per cent. One observes that free labour and money were the only significant contributions rural people were willing to make towards community development.

The proportion of the respondents that was willing to contribute cash was rather disappointing. Yet we made the effort to test the hypothesis that there is a significant relationship between willingness to contribute money toward community development and the level of one's income and access to credit. The assumption underlying this hypothesis is that since production credit leads to improved incomes and higher standard of living, the ability to contribute cash towards community development is, to a large extent, dependent on one's income and access to credit. The hypothesis was tested in two parts, namely — (1) relationship between level of income and contribution of cash towards community development and (2) relationship between access to credit and contribution of cash towards community development.

In testing the first part of this hypothesis, we used the levels of income for 1989 (Table 4.14) as in our fourth hypothesis. The results shown in Table 30 indicate that the relationship is significant at 0.01 level of probability. We then measured the direction of relationship and found a weak positive correlation between the two variables with $Q = 0.4$. The second part of the hypothesis.

The results in Table 31 show that the relationship is not significant at the 0.01 level, though there is also weak positive correlation between the two variables with $Q = 0.4$. We can, therefore, infer that even though the relationship is significant in the first part of the hypothesis, the positive correlation is too weak for us to conclude that the willingness of rural people to contribute money towards community development depends on the level of one's income. Similarly there is no significant correlation between access to credit and willingness to contribute funds towards community development.

TABLE 30

**Relationship Between Level of Income and Willingness of Respondents
to Contribute Money towards Community Development**

Contribution of Money	Level of Income		
	High	Low	Total
Yes	40	25	65
No	65	93	158
Total	105	118	223

$\chi^2 = 7.702$, $\alpha = 0.01$, P is significant and Q = 0.4.

TABLE 31

**Relationship Between Access to Credit and Willingness
of Respondents to Contribute Money Towards
Community Development**

Contribution of Money	Access to Credit		
	High	Low	Total
Yes	52	16	68
No	107	70	177
Total	159	86	245

$\chi^2 = 5.574$, $\alpha = 0.01$, P is not significant and Q = 0.4.

We further asked respondents to indicate how much money they could contribute per annum towards community development. Table 32 presents the frequency distribution of the responses. "Any amount levied by the community" with 27.5 per cent of the cases is clearly the modal level of contributions. This is followed by ¢1,000.00 (24.6 per cent) and ¢500.00 (21.7 per cent). The fact that over a quarter of the respondents were willing to contribute "any amount levied by community" was an indication that given the resources, rural people would contribute money towards the improvement of facilities in their communities.

TABLE 32

**Amount Respondents were Willing to Contribute Towards
Communtiy Development per Annum**

Amount (¢)	Number	Percentage
Less than 500.00	8	11.6
500.00	15	21.7
1000.00	17	24.6
2000.00	2	2.9
3000.00	1	1.4
4000.00	0	0.0
5000.00	1	1.4
Over 5000.00	6	8.7
Any amount levied by community	19	27.5
Total	69	100.0

6.2.4   *The Contribution of Credit Institutions Towards Rural Development*
We have noted the role of the rural financial intermediaries in the credit
delivery system for the support of the economic activities in the rural areas.
In this connection, we asked credit institutions to indicate what they
considered to be the most important areas of activity to which they would
contribute to enhance rural development in the Keta district. The results
from the four banks are considered individually.

The management of the Ghana Commercial Bank at Keta indicated
that their contribution to rural development was the granting of loans to
fishermen, Canoe Fishermen Society and fishmongers. This contribution to
the fisheries sector of agriculture is important for the development of this
sector in the district, for it enables borrowers to procure the necessary
inputs for their work. The Ghana Commercial Bank at Abor named granting
of loans to rice farmers at Afife and its assistance in the disbursement of
World Vision International Funds for development projects at Atiavi, Anyako,
Abɔlɔve, Nɔlɔfi and Asadame. The Ghana Cooperative Bank at Anloga
mentioned the granting of loans to farmers and fishermen to buy production
assets such as canoe, nets, seeds and farm tools as the most important
contribution to rural development.

Finally, the Volta Premier Rural Bank (VPRB) mentioned five main contributions to rural development. The most important of her contributions was the granting of commodity loans to individuals in the form of fishing gear (nets, ropes and outboard motors), building materials (cement, roofing sheets), farm implements (maize-shellers, incubators and tools), cornmill and bicycles. The bank also provided cash loans to small-scale producers such as farmers, fishermen, fishsmokers and craftsmen. Thirdly, the bank made donations to schools and hospitals for their structural development. Fourthly, the bank had a special transportation loan which was granted to reliable drivers or commercial transport owners to buy vehicles on a "work-and-pay" basis. This, in addition to vehicle rehabilitation loans, had brought many more vehicles on the roads, thus, easing the transportation problem in the catchment area of the bank. Finally, the bank had bought a tractor for the Keta District Assembly for carting materials to its development project sites and relief items to victims of natural disasters.

From the foregoing, we can conclude that the contributions made by the VPRB towards rural development surpassed those of the commercial banks in the district. This has been made possible not only because of its special role as a rural (development) bank but also because, as a unit bank, it is not subject to any control from a "head office". We also noted that all the banks gave loans to farmers and fishermen in order to boost the agricultural sector which occupies a major part of the economic activities of the rural communities. For this reason, therefore, the banks contribute to rural development.

6.3   Development Priorities of Rural People

In the past, the provision of socio-economic infrastructure was brought down to rural people by the central government. This top-down approach to rural development not only failed to consider what the priorities of the various localities might be but also excluded the rural interest groups from the management of the projects (Agyeman 1987: 99). The projects that resulted from this approach, therefore, tended to be white-elephants which often collapse as a result of lack of interest and support by the rural communities. The involvement of rural people in the planning, financing, execution and management of social development projects has been noted to be very crucial for sustainable rural development. It is against this background that we examined the development priorities of rural people.

6.3.1   Ranking of Facilities (Needs) for which Respondents would
Contribute Towards Development
We recall in section 6.2.4 that the entire sample would want to contribute more towards community development if their incomes increase. Respondents were then asked the question: "If you were to contribute money or materials towards the improvement of your community, what three items

in order of priority would you want to have?". The results of the ranking are shown in Table 33. It shows that with only one exception, the four localities did not differ much in their development priorities. Three localities — Vodza, Fiahor and Abor ranked the provision of pipe-borne water or well as their number one priority. This was expected because lack of good drinking water has been noted in the three localities as a major problem (see section 3.5.1, 3.5.3 and 3.5.4 of Chapter 3). On the other hand, Agbledomi-Dzita ranked the construction of good roads as her number one priority. This was also anticipated as it was the most inaccessible of the four localities (section 3.5.2). The second and third priority needs of the four localities were as follows: Vodza — public toilet/latrine and health centre; Agbledomi-Dzita — health centre and public toilet/latrine; and Abor — market and electricity, all in that order.

TABLE 33

Respondents' Ranking of Community Needs by Locality

Need	Total Score and Rank Order by Locality[1]							
	Vodza		Agbledomi-Dzita		Fiahor		Abor	
	Score	Rank	Score	Rank	Score	Rank	Score	Rank
Public Toilet/Lat.	77	(2)	41	(3)	7	(4)	96	(4)
Pipe-borne water/well	108	(1)	7	(8)	50	(1)	220	(1)
Good roads	19	(4)	150	(1)	31	(2)	5	(8)
Electricity	9	(5)	35	(4)	7	(4)	131	(3)
Health centre	44	(3)	105	(2)	15	(3)	24	(5)
2nd Cycle School	3	(7)	19	(5)	0	(9)	14	(7)
Market	0	(8)	3	(10)	3	(7)	0	(9)
Agric. Ext. Office	0	(8)	3	(10)	3	(7)	0	(9)
Agric. Inputs Depot	0	(8)	5	(9)	0	(9)	0	(9)
Others[2]	7	(6)	13	(7)	6	(6)	16	(6)

Notes: 1. The needs are scored as: First position = 3, Second position = 2, and Third position = 1. The frequencies were multiplied by the rates to obtain the score at each position. Total score is, therefore, the sum of the scores for the three positions.
2. Includes: library, bank, post office, community centre, public transport services and football park.

It was only at Abor that market and electricity supply came into the top three — an indication of growing urban traits. Secondly, my own observation and informal chats with community leaders show that the rankings provided by the respondents were the true reflection of the needs and aspirations of the four localities. Finally, the distribution re-emphasizes the point that rural development planning must be a joint-venture between the government and the rural people. This would ensure a more efficient allocation of resources to the priority needs of the people and enhance their involvement and support.

6.3.2   Government's Protection of Rural People Against Natural Disasters

The development priorities of rural people are often determined by ecological conditions. These conditions are also exacerbated by the prevalence of natural disasters which may cause destruction of facilities and bring untold hardship to rural people. Thus, the number one priority need for Vodza is "pipe-borne water" because the old water pipes had long been destroyed both by sea erosion and lagoon flooding. Agbledomi-Dzita places "road" as the number one priority while Fiahor makes it the number two priority just because sections of the existing roads have been rendered unmotorable by flood waters. In view of our observation in section 3.4.1 of Chapter 3 that the Keta district has been a natural disaster prone area, the people always looked up to the government for protection against these natural disasters.

In this regard, we asked respondents whether they thought that rural people were adequately protected by the government against natural disasters. The result indicated 51.6 per cent positive response, 47.2 per cent negative and 1.2 per cent indifferent. Those who gave positive responses were further asked to mention up to four (4) forms of protection government provided to rural people in times of natural disasters. Table 34 presents the frequency distribution of multiple responses. It indicates that rural people recognized the role being played by government towards disaster relief. Three of the most frequently mentioned forms of government protection were: "supply of relief food items" (67.2 per cent), supply of relief clothing and blankets (57 per cent) and resettlement of victims (45.3 per cent)". These, in fact, were noted to be the three basic necessities of life — food, clothings and shelter.

Those who gave negative responses, on the other hand, were asked to mention up to four (4) forms of protection they would want government to provide against natural disasters. Incidentally, the same items in Table 34 came up again for mention. We present the multiple response distribution in Table 35 where three most frequently expected forms of protection from the government by the people were: supply of relief food items (41.7 per cent), provision of building materials to victims (38.9 per cent) and provision of loans to victims to buy fresh inputs for farming (37 per cent).

Here again, two of the basic necessities of life, food and shelter were viewed as the most urgently required protection government should provide for victims of natural disasters.

TABLE 34

**Nature of Government Protection of Rural People
Against Natural Disasters (In Percentage)**

Nature of Protection	Multiple Responses (N = 128)		
	Yes	No	Total
Provision of building materials to victims	25.0	75.0	100.0
Resettlement of affected persons	45.3	54.7	100.0
Supply of Agricultural inputs to victims	15.6	84.4	100.0
Provision of loans to victims to buy fresh inputs	32.0	68.0	100.0
Supply of relief food items	67.2	32.8	100.0
Supply of relief clothings/ blankets	57.0	43.0	100.0
Whatever government feels appropriate	2.3	97.7	100.0

6.4   Conclusion

In this chapter, we have shown the need to mobilize rural resources of savings, cash contributions and communal labour for rural development. It was asserted that the extent to which rural people were willing to contribute cash (money) towards the social development of their communities was not dependent upon their income levels and their access to credit to improve their production capacities. We have also demonstrated that each locality has its own basket of priority needs. Thus, we observed the need to fully involve rural people in development project planning, implementation and management. In the final chapter of this thesis, we shall summarize the main findings and draw some conclusions and implications of this study for planning and policy decision making.

TABLE 35

**Nature of Protection Respondents Expect Government
to Provide to Rural People Against Disasters
(In Percentages)**

Nature of Protection	Multiple Responses (N = 108)[1]		
	Yes	No	Total
Provision of building materials to victims	38.9	61.1	100.0
Resettlement of affected persons	33.3	66.7	100.0
Supply of Agricultural inputs to victims	13.9	86.1	100.0
Provision of loans to victims to buy fresh inputs	37.0	63.0	100.0
Supply of relief food items	41.7	58.3	100.0
Supply of relief clothings/ blankets			
Whatever government feels appropriate	17.7	84.3	100.0

Note: [1]Non-response = 9.

REFERENCES

Adams, D. W. and R. C. Vogel 1986. "Rural Financial Markets in low-income Countries: Recent Controversies and lessons"; *World Development,* Vol. 14, No. 4 pp. 477–487.

Agyeman, D. K. 1987. *Education for Rural Development: Exploring the Views, Expectation and Recommendations of Rural People,* Unpublished Survey Report, Cape Coast.

Brown, C. K. 1981/82. "Rural Deprivation and Underdevelopment in Ghana: The Views of the Students of the University of Ghana", *Ghana Journal of Sociology,* Vol. xiv, No. 1 pp. 27–60.

Brown, C. K. 1984. *Social Structure and Poverty in Selected Rural Communities in Ghana,* ISSER Poverty Study Series, No. 6, University of Ghana, Legon (Mimeo).

Ewusi, Kodwo 1978. *Planning for the Neglected Rural Poor in Ghana,* New Times Corporation, Accra.

Kurihara, K. K. 1970. *Monetary Theory and Public Policy,* George Allen and Unwin, London.

Chapter 7

USES OF SOCIAL RESEARCH, SUMMARY AND CONCLUSION

USES OF SOCIAL RESEARCH

In all social life, in the civic society, as well as in societal institutions, social facts are needed to help decision-makers. Individuals and social groups as well as social institutions must be guided by facts and by informed statements. In social life, we constantly embark on developmental projects. People must be involved in initiating and in understanding projects, in building their communities, in going about their day to day occupational activities. In all these rounds of activities, social facts obtained from research work are the guiding principles for sustainable development projects.

Rural farmers, fishermen and women and indeed, all categories of workers should benefit from the end results of social research. Farmers would like to know how to improve their yields. Fishermen would like to know where to obtain their fishing resources. Market women would like to know from where to obtain their products at the best prices.

Traditional political authority leaders, chiefs and their sub-chiefs would also benefit from the results of relevant social research. It will go a long way to help them to improve upon the positive aspects of what they have and to discard negative practices. It will help them to engage in projects to maintain their communities as well as to improve the chieftaincy institution. In this age of decentralization of political authority, the district assembly members would definitely need reliable and valid information to help them steer the affairs of their districts. In so doing, the discussions they engage in will be relevant to the needs of their communities and they will be able to be specific in their discussions based on reliable and valid information.

It is precisely in this direction that meaningful social research must be seen as useful and be pursued in rural districts to help minimize ignorance which tends to be anti-social and anti-productive and thus, cost ineffective in the rural setting. Changes in the school curriculum in rural areas, for example, must be introduced to interest school-leavers to do research work and to stay in the rural districts. We need also to introduce in the school curriculum, relevant science and research subjects to help school-leavers to bridge the gap between the home and the school. It is hoped that with a relevant school curriculum, school-leavers would begin to appreciate the need to research into the environment to affect the lives of traditional men and women. Indeed, we need to build this country upon the good aspects of their lives and their activities and methods of approach to their work. It is through research work that we can improve upon the solid foundations of our institutions. Research orientation would make the school-leavers more appreciative to help to build the society through their own creativity and experience. We need not produce school-leavers who tend to be so distant and arrogantly far removed from their own reality. Such people tend to boycott what is going on in their real society. Research work and the uses of research knowledge are essential elements in nation building.

Now that all the districts are going to be connected to the national electricity grid and leading roads and feeder roads are being built in rural districts, we expect school-leavers to be interested in staying in their districts to create the needed small-scale jobs to the benefit of the people in rural areas. With the creation of the district assembly we should be guided by relevant research studies to help us to strengthen rural development.

The point we need to make is that our educational system whether modern or traditional must be seen to be nurtured continually in research orientation conducted in the real situation so as to meet with the rural developmental needs. It must be functionally oriented without loosing site of its theoretical and cross cultural perspectives. Social facts will help to bridge the gap which had existed between the home and the school since the colonial times. We can help in bridging the gap from the following specific suggestions:

1. In primary schools, knowledgeable citizens in traditional institutions such as our chiefs, our industrious farmers and artisans must be invited to share their social knowledge with the school authorities and their pupils. It is through such an interaction that the uses of social research can be seen.

2. Practical fieldwork must be undertaken in the actual job setting to make meaningful for pupils and students what they

have obtained from their classroom theoretical instructions. The community at large will benefit.

3.   Wherever possible, practical research demonstration work must be situated in the real world of work experience. For example, if a pupil is expected to do a research work in carpentry, he or she must be attached to the real world of carpenters to work and to collect reliable and valid information to help them appreciate reality and to acquire the tenets of the scientific method.

4.   In all rural schools, teachers must interact with the elders in their communities by interesting them to be involved in the selection and dissemination of research knowledge.

The private sector must also help to institutionalize the need for social research for the youth in the rural districts, because in the final analysis they are the main beneficiaries of the products of social research. It is through research interaction of this nature that effective production, buying and selling as well as market trends would be made known to the benefit of the private sector investors and to the rural community at large. No one should say that this form of education is expensive because it goes without saying that ignorance is more expensive than education. In this context, whoever puts money into research training and into the uses of research knowledge would have clearly brought the future to the threshold of his/her doorstep. In this sense, it is men and women who change things, who change technology and who can change working methods. Indeed, it is only through research knowledge that we can have sustainable transformation and can manage social change.

A purposeful social research education, therefore, is that type of education that brings out the best in the individual to relate and to appreciate his or her own environment of which he or she is part. We must know what is going on in our environment. We must begin to understand the social structural arrangement of our society. We must study the type and nature of people who live in the society, their demographic structure, why they do things and the way they do things must be understood. We must understand the institutional networks of our society, the existing occupational structures, patterns of marriage and family systems, religious affiliations, economic issues, health institutions and in fact the entire societal institutional networks must be understood. It is through social research work that we can build on them in a sustainable and in developmental ways. This will involve a careful study of each district in order to discover the potentiality of each district. We need to research each district to find out, its structure, the disease pattern, types of occupation and the nature of the soil and vegetation, the existing institutions, and type of social organization. Studies of this nature should be provided on each district as a profile so that in the end policy-makers and decision-makers at all levels would get an intelligible insight into the social and economic situation in the rural districts, to help to develop the districts.

The young ones must be introduced to purposeful research education which must begin at the roots. It is only then that we can begin to appreciate what is happening in other parts of the world. Purposeful education is rooted in research orientation to help us to appreciate the reconstruction of our reality. It helps us to develop our society from the grassroots and to bring us in line with the developmental trend of the vast majority of our people who hitherto had been left out. It helps us to come face to face with the real meaning of social life and how to improve it.

This real meaning of research work education will help us to appreciate the individual and to harness his or her potentiality through the various opportunities available for learning. The learning experiences are within the environment. These experiences will go a long way to help the individual to broaden his cultural horizon. It is for this reason that there is the need for research educators to deepen the meaning of education to include a well grounded knowledge of the person's appreciation of the society with a view to improving it. Research education must not limit the individual or must not be limited "only to those who have passed through the universities". This form of education is indeed of limited value and does not justify the real meaning of a purposeful education. Research education must not exclude a large sector of our population who are living in the rural areas. They have indeed contributed much to the development of our country and must help with new knowledge through research. There are many people within our society who have contributed to the development of our society but have never set foot into our formal schools. On the other hand, there are many people who have attended formal schools and colleges yet have contributed very little and have poor knowledge of what the reality is in appreciating what goes on in their own environment. This situation does not augur well for the development of our rural areas, thus, the need to involve all people to appreciate the need to use research information.

Traditional and modern ways of education will be bridged through reliable information. We need to incorporate the good ways of traditional educational model into our modern curriculum to come up with relevant and purposeful education because traditional experiences are guided by reality. In the rural setting, for example, the child is evaluated constantly by adults, by his parents and by other members of the household. At an appreciable age, when the child is old enough to understand basic instructions and physically able, he or she starts practical lessons to help to become a productive person. A child follows the instructions of parents. The girl child begins to learn her duties in housekeeping, in keeping the body clean, washing, ironing and other related domestic duties. She is supervised by her relatives in an informal setting. A boy learns from his parents in a similar way. If the father is a carpenter, he learns to trade in carpentry. He also learns the manners, the attitudes, the values and the expected roles and duties he is to play from his social models.

When of age biologically, the traditional child is also of age socially. There is no gap between the biological and social age. It is through this form of broad based education that the traditional child acquires his or her status and role to be productive and relevant in the society. The hoe, the bow and arrow, the agricultural knowledge, carpentry, arts and craft, marketing wisdom are examples of the outcome of traditional training and knowledge which we must improve upon through research work.

In modern terms, the child goes to school to learn in an abstract way. In most cases, what he learns is of no immediate functional benefit to his environment. This gap so created between what is taught at school and what is real in the society has, in fact, been recognized by many well meaning educators but they find it uneasy to bridge the gap. As a result, we have created a situation in which those who had not been through the formal walls of educational system are looked down upon. This misconception of education should be corrected through social dialogue by bringing in knowledgeable traditional people into the school system to instruct the youth whenever it is appropriate and to encourage them to study their social environment to help them to understand their communities.

In functional terms, the reality of the situation is that there is the need to bridge the gap between the school and the rural community. We need also to revise our thinking and discard the old fashioned situation where those who have been to formal schools tend to think that they are the only custodians of knowledge. This view is fallacious and it is malicious as well, and can be corrected through research work.

Anyway one looks at the problem, it becomes even clearer to say those who had not been to school had remained very creative and had contributed enormously to the development of this country because they understand the system they are operating in. Take a look at our farmers, our fishermen, carpenters, tailors and fitters, for example. Not even the doubting Thomases would deny the knowledge and skills of these men and women. Take a look at our traditional statesmen and linguists in the traditional system, they have helped to build an enduring system. We must build upon their knowledge and skills through research work.

It is precisely in this context that the participation of our traditional people should be sought in the development of our communities. Our young men and women can only learn, through humility which comes to us through the willingness to study what we do not know form the facts and figures.

I submit that the properly educated person must be a humble person and must be committed to research work and respect for reliable and valid information as the basis to build a sound and a viable society.

SUMMARY AND CONCLUSION

We discussed the stages involved in the research process in this book and we confined our discussion to the main problems and issues in rural social research. We argued that Ghana, like many other developing countries, has a large sector of its population living in rural and outlying villages. For this reason, the social scientist must take note of the norms, values and the social organization of the people whenever he initiates a research study. Any social scientist who decides to study in rural areas must undertake a pilot study to gain an insight into the cultural environment of the people.

The social scientist usually goes to the field to study social phenomena in its natural setting. Unlike the laboratory method in which the setting is controlled, the field survey method poses many problems. It is not easy for example to define the operational field, to take a representative sample and to use field data collecting techniques in order to x-ray the social reality of the people. In this context, we discussed the issues of errors, sampling and non-sampling errors. The first type of error arises because of the inability of the investigator to "know" the field and to consult a colleague or a sampling statistician. The second type of research error arises if the investigator selects data collecting procedures without first getting to know the people's way of life. The tools of social research must be selected only when the investigator is well acquainted with the people so that the methods will suit the conditions of the rural people. Failure to take these factors into consideration tends to affect the quality of the information, the representativeness of the sample and the field response rate.

The field helpers, assistants, informants and other people who are usually called upon to assist the investigator must be trained and selected carefully, in terms of their understanding of the research method and their knowledge of the field situation. In training, they must be schooled towards the aims and aspirations of the research. All the research questions and other key concepts must be translated into the local language. They must also be trained to interpret in a uniform manner "open-ended" type of questions.

It was pointed out that the use of questionnaire method poses many problems. Non-literate people may find it difficult to respond to formal questions; they may feel shy to answer, in a specific way, sensitive questions. The elderly people may find it unusual to answer questions from young interviewers. Again, we mentioned that the questionnaire method involves other complex data processing stages, for example, coding and computer analysis. The researcher using such procedures needs to have well trained research assistants and will also need the availability of the relevant data processing resources. In the industrial nations, computers and other research resources are usually available whereas in the developing countries, these sophisticated tools may not be available or may be in limited use. Universities in Ghana and research institutions now have adequate computer workstations. Therefore, within rural oriented cultures, research scientists must be aware of the limitations and adapt their field operations to suit local conditions.

The scientific method is an organized method, useful in collecting, processing and accumulating knowledge. Built into it is the humility to question spurious material and to update knowledge. For this reason, we argued that social scientists must use the scientific method. In comparative terms, the methods and the area of operation of the social scientists are not the same as in the physical sciences. Nevertheless, this is not to argue that we should not use the scientific method. Rather, we must endeavour to improve on the tools of data processing in order to present intelligent image of our societies.

As observed by T. S. Eliot in his *Little Gidding* (Four Quarters, New York: Harcourt Brace and Co., 1945).

We shall not cease from exploration,
And the end of all our exploring
Will be to arrive where we started.
And know the place for the first time.

BIBLIOGRAPHY

Addo, N. O., G. Benneh, J. M. Assimeng, J. Kudadjie, S. A. Danquah and P. A. Twumasi (1975). *Impact of Tourism on Social Life in Ghana* (Accra: Ghana Tourist Board, unpublished manuscript.

Babbie, Earl (1982a) *Science and Morality*. Los Angeles: University of California Press.

Babbie, Earl (1982b) *Social Research for Consumers*. Belmont: C.A. Wodsworth Press.

Babbie, Earl (1990) *Survey Research Methods*. Belmont: C.A. Wodsworth Press.

Babbie, Earl (1995) *The Practice of Social Research* (7th Edition), New York: International Thomson Publishing Company.

Blalock, M. (1960) *Social Statistics*. New York: Mcgraw Hill.

Biesanz, John and Mavis Biesanz (1969) *Introduction to Sociology,* New Jersey: Prentice-Hall, Inc.

Blumer, Herbert (1970) "Methodological Principles of Empirical Science" in Normal K. Denzin (ed.), *Sociological Methods: A Source Book*. London: Butterworth, pp. 20–33.

Boruch Robert and Jean S. Cecil (1979) *Assuring the Confidentiality of Social Research Data*. Philadelphia: University of Pennsylvania Press.

Cohen, M. R. and E. Nagel (1934) *An Introduction to Logic and Scientific Method*. New York: Harcourt Brace, chap. 12.

Cole, Stephen (1980) *The Sociological Method: An Introduction to the Science of Sociology*. Boston: Houghton Mifflin.

Durkheim, Emile (1966) *The Division of Labour in Society*. New York: The Free Press, Third Printing.

Hsin-Pao, Yang (1955) *Fact-Finding with Rural People*. FAO, Publication.

Jahoda, Gustav (1954) "The Social Background of a West African Student Population", *British Journal of Sociology* Vol. 5, No. 4 and Vol. 6, No. 1.

Kish, Leslie (1967) *Survey Sampling*. New York: John Wiley.

Nukunya, G. K. and P. A. Twumasi (1975) *A Study of Traditional Attitudes Towards Health, Diseases and Family Planning in Four Ghanaian Communities*. Unpublished monograph, Population Dynamics Programme, University of Ghana, Legon.

Riley, Matilda (1964) *Sociological Research*. New York: Maclo.

Sorokin, Pitirim, A. (1962) *Social and Cultural Mobility,* New York: The Free Press of Glencoe.

Twumasi, P. A. (1975) *Medical Systems in Ghana: A Study in Medical Sociology*. Tema: Ghana Publishing Corporation.

Weber, Max (1956) "Science as a Vocation" in Gerth, Hans and C. Wright Mills trans (eds). *From Max Weber: Essays in Sociology,* New York: Oxford University Press.

Index